# *Strange Deaths*

# *Strange Deaths*

## *More than 375*
## *Freakish Fatalities*

COMPILED BY PAUL SIEVEKING
& IAN SIMMONS

WITH ADDITIONAL MATERIAL BY
VAL STEVENSON

ILLUSTRATIONS BY ED TRAQUINO

BARNES
& NOBLE
BOOKS

NEW YORK

*Publisher's Note:* British units of measurement are used throughout the text. It may be helpful for the reader to know that one stone is equal to fourteen pounds.

Originally published as
*The Fortean Times Book of More Strange Deaths*

Copyright © 1998 by Fortean Times/John Brown Publishing

This edition published by Barnes & Noble, Inc.,
by arrangement with John Brown Publishing

2000 Barnes & Noble Books

ISBN 0-7607-1947-0

Printed and bound in the United States of America

05 06 07 08 09 MP 9 8 7

FG

# CONTENTS

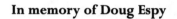

**In memory of Doug Espy**

# INTRODUCTION

Death and taxes (or, as Ian misheard as a child, taxis) are supposed to be the only constants in life and, as Peter Greenaway has one of his characters point out in his film *Drowning by Numbers*, "A great many things are dying very violently all the time." Looking at our files, one could equally say: "A great many things are dying very strangely all the time" – enough for us to have accumulated a thick file of strange deaths in the short time since the first *Fortean Times Book of Strange Deaths* was published. This has been the most popular of all our compilations, so it seemed the time was right to gather this new material together and produce a sequel, and here it is. Drawing on Paul's published *Strange Death* columns and the vast pile of clippings which we just don't have the room for in the magazine, this compilation surveys the vast variety of unusual exits the Grim Reaper seems to have devised to inflict upon humanity to keep himself amused.

But for the grace of something or other, Ian could have ended up as an entry in these pages himself (a few years back, he narrowly escaped that most fortean death – being crushed by his collection of books and clippings after some shelving he had incompetently constructed and overloaded collapsed as he searched for a volume on it). From the ludicrous to the sickening, there seems to be no end to the new ways that can be found to kill people. When leading American fortean Mark Chorvinsky spoke at the 1998 *Fortean Times* UnConvention on Grim Reaper sightings, the idea that an entity might actually exist which was dreaming these exits up did not come as a surprise.

We'd love to put our hand on our (still beating) hearts and say that every tale told herein is one hundred per cent true, but alas we cannot. Our stories have been culled from newspapers and magazines worldwide, sent to us by the dedicated and unflagging band of clipsters who provide the lifeblood of *FT*, giving us full access to the weirdness chronicled by the *Victoria (BC) Times-Colonist, Saginaw News, Times of Malta, Hong Kong Standard* and many more, so our information can only be as good as our sources. Alas, the standards of journalism are not consistent, and many papers are not above exaggerating for comic effect, recycling old stories with names and locations changed or removed, claiming hoary urban legends as fact, or even making things up from scratch. Much as we would like to, we do not have the resources to follow up and verify every story we receive. We have, however, detailed all our sources at the back of the book, so you can decide for yourself how reliable you think the story is. Where we think something is an urban legend we have mentioned it in the text (I mean, *four tons* of toenails – come on!).

We hope you find this as entertaining to read as we did to compile. Live long and prosper!

**Paul Sieveking & Ian Simmons**

# *I'll Get Out of This If It Kills Me!*

**... is the lament of many a bored worker, but for some it comes all too tragically true.**

**THREE U.S. NAVY** airmen died in a bizarre ærial mooning incident in 1995. The two pilots and a navigator were flying alongside a second warplane when they stripped off all their clothes and pressed their backsides to the cockpit canopy as a joke. However, they also took off their oxygen masks, without which they rapidly lost consciousness, leaving their aircraft to plunge to the ground and killing everyone aboard. In another incident, a U.S. Air Force transport plane crashed when the pilot let his wife fly it while on a 'spousal orientation flight' designed to help wives learn about their husbands' jobs. The causes of these accidents were allegedly covered up by embarrassed U.S. military authorities.

**ALSO STRIPPING OFF** were secret lovers Frauke Punz, 22, and Ulf Lech, 31, who worked together in a steelworks in Essen, Germany. As their works closed for its summer break, they sneaked into a lift for an illicit sex session. But while they reached the heights of passion, the electricity was turned off, leaving them trapped between floors in total darkness, while everyone went on holiday. Their mummified bodies were found by a security man four weeks later when the factory returned to work. Unable to raise the alarm by hammering on the walls of the lift, fitness fanatic Ulf had tried to climb the cables, but they were too greasy and he had to go back. The couple died an agonising death of dehydration in the midst of the empty factory, leaving a final note on a scrap of paper reading: "We are at the end of our strength, but our love for each other is eternal. But why ..." Although single, they had kept their romance secret because they feared bosses would move them to other offices.

**FRANK NELSON**, 26, died almost instantly on 22 September 1997 when he fell into a vat mixing polymers at a Nalley Valley plastics factory near Tacoma, Washington. He was pouring colouring into the cylindrical 3ft x 5ft vat when he fell in and was sliced by revolving blades. Also for the chop was an Israeli soldier on leave from combat duty who was sucked into a giant dough-mixer and kneaded to death at Jerusalem's Mystic Pizza. A co-worker at the pizzeria said that Moshe Dor-On, 21, had reached into the mixer to pull up dough from the bottom when he was sucked in. And Armando Merola, 51, died after falling into an 8ft-high mincing machine he was cleaning at the Beni Foods factory in Tongwell near Milton Keynes. "The paddles inside were jammed by his body. He was still alive," said a fellow worker. Another worker switched off the power, but the machine started again, crushing Merola.

**CHEF** Juan Ruiz was stabbed through the heart with uncooked spaghetti strands when 150mph winds hit his restaurant in

Mexico City. Two months later, a young employee of the Bennett Food Factory in the Bronx, New York, died instantly when he fell head-first into an industrial dough-mixer making macaroni and was impaled by the mixing blades.

**SALESMAN** Rico Vogt choked to death in Pisa, Italy, when his tie got tangled round the blades of a food mixer he was demonstrating to a crowd in a shopping centre.

**WHEN** a window dresser collapsed face-down on a bed and died at work, shoppers in Johannesburg thought he was a mannequin. The truth emerged three days later when a passer-by complained the display was in bad taste.

**VETERAN** saké brewer Masakichi Kindaichi, 58, was pouring fermented rice into a 6ft-deep metal tank in Fukushima, Japan, when he lost his balance and fell into the vat. By the time fellow workers noticed he was missing, he had been overcome by the fumes and suffocated. Also getting tanked were three 18-year-olds doing national service in the Ukraine. They were sent to clean a 12ft-deep underground food container in Charkov and were fatally overcome by pickled cabbage fumes, as was a 48-year-old worker who went to their rescue. There was another terminal tank in Ireland: a Co Armagh man got into trouble while he was cleaning out a slurry tank on a farm near Markethill. A fellow worker tried to rescue him, but both died. Elsewhere, a flood of sewage in Shchebekino, Russia, drowned three sanitation workers doing routine maintenance at a sewage plant.

**FIVE** workers at a Thailand factory were electrocuted when a live lead from a radio fell into a pickled mango storage tank. Police in Udon Thani said workers were removing mangoes at the time. One was electrocuted instantly and the others died as they tried to help their colleagues.

**ACCOUNTANT** Arthur Roberts lost his temper when he accidentally wiped his firm's sales figures off his computer. He threw the machine out of his window in Brisbane, Australia ... and killed pedestrian Peter Mullins. He was charged with manslaughter.

**THE CHIEF ACCOUNTANT** from the failed Japanese brokerage Yamaichi Securities Co worked without a break for 14 days from a week before the crash – Japan's largest post-war failure – and did not leave the office during that period. The 38-year-old man finally went home in Tokyo on 27 November 1997 and was found dead in bed the next morning. Verdict: fatigue.

**HASHIEM ZAYED**, 59, a short-order cook, and waitress Helen Menicou, 47, had worked together at the Pine Crest Diner in San Francisco for 22 fractious years. On 23 July 1997 she publicly scolded him for making poached eggs for a customer when it was not on the menu. This was the last straw: the next day he came to work and shot her dead.

**A ROW** between rival collectors of bat excrement, a valuable resource used in organic fertiliser, left five dead and two seriously injured after a home-made grenade was tossed into the mouth of a bat cave in the Pak Chong district of Nakhon Ratchasima province in Thailand on 2 April 1998. A survivor told police the group was leaving the cave with seven sacks-full when the explosion ripped through them. A rival gang of dungmen was suspected.

**A BLACKSMITH** in a Russian village was killed by an explosion after hammering on a cannon shell he had used as an anvil for 10 years. He had been told it was a training dummy.

**GREENKEEPER** Ronnie Mitchell, who worked at Bradley Hall golf club near Elland, West Yorks, fell foul of a giant petrol-driven lawnmower. His jacket caught round the axle and dragged him to death, trapping him between a wheel and one of the huge cutting arms.

**MORRIS HONEY,** a 55-year-old Oxford University groundsman, was run over and killed by a two-ton roller. He was digging a weed out of the cricket field while the roller was still moving (if he had stopped it, it would have left an indentation) when his foot got caught. After the inquest, his widow said that Morris had "lived and died for cricket." David Duffee, 35, also fell foul of a steamroller. He died on a Cape Town, South Africa, building site when he jumped to escape a truck and was run over by a steamroller.

**MEXICAN** roadworker José Alvarez lost his job painting yellow lines after he ordered his gang to paint them over a dead man. "I thought he was drunk and passed out," Alvarez explained. "We didn't mean any harm."

**WINDOW CLEANER** Thomas Scott fell 10 feet to his death when a frustrated colleague kicked his ladder out from under him during a row over his drinking. Scott was arguing with his colleague of 17 years, Michael Tibbins, about his drunken behaviour at a christening the previous day when Tibbins kicked the ladder, causing Scott, 46, to crash to the ground, fracturing his skull. He died two days later.

**WHILE** trying to shoot a cow, Farmer Roger Voyle, 33, failed to hit the animal, but managed to shoot one of his farmhands. After agreeing to slaughter a heifer belonging to a neighbour, Voyle borrowed a cut-down sports rifle from a professional slaughterman and tried to kill the animal with farmhand Michael Spencer's help. The gun was meant to be fired with the barrel touching the cow's head. Voyle missed with the first shot, then reloaded and missed again, shooting Mr Spencer, 51, through the heart.

**A GARAGE WORKER** was scrubbed to death in Melbourne, Australia, in a bizarre accident with a car wash. Eccentric Reggie Peabody liked to ride the brushes when business was slow, but something went wrong and when the wash stopped his colleagues found Peabody's lifeless body still clinging to the giant brush.

**A PEASANT** in Yunnan, south-west China, was sentenced to death after being found guilty of killing five people by rolling rocks onto a road in the hope that they would damage passing vehicles which he could later fix for money.

**ASTRONOMER** Marc Aaronson, 37, best known for his work on the age and size of the universe, was crushed to death between a door and the 150-ton revolving telescope dome at Kitt Peak Observatory, Arizona.

**SECURITY** firm owner Vittorio Cavaletti was assassinated by his latest product, an armoured car, when the heavy door slammed shut on his neck after he kicked it because it was jammed open. "He was dead before we could release him," said firemen in Mantova, Italy.

# *Fatal Coincidence*

**In death, as in life, curious correlations are rife.**

**THE DAUGHTER** of a woman who was killed when she fell down a cliff-face blowhole in 1992 fell down the same blowhole five years later. She and another young woman were swept into the Pacific Ocean near Sydney.

**KENNETH STEVENS**, 19, was killed when his motorbike struck a bullock on a country road near his home in Sourton, near Okehampton, Devon. It was almost a duplicate of the accident in the same spot eight years before which had killed his father David. Driving home in thick fog, his car struck a bullock in the road and he was killed outright.

**TWO MOTORCYCLISTS** died within minutes of each other in identical accidents in Pinhoe Road, Exeter. The first rider, 20-year-old Neil Walters, smashed into the back of a parked lorry at full speed on his 100cc Suzuki and died of terrible head injuries. As police were leaving the scene, pensioner Leslie Sanders, 71, riding his brand-new 90cc Honda with only 44 miles on the clock, did exactly the same, also dying of head injuries. Police said: "The lorry was not illegally parked and the street lights were on. But the road was wet and it was raining steadily."

**EIGHTEEN** Nigerians died when a fuel tanker crashed through a police check-point in Lagos, hit a bus and burst into flames in a repetition of an identical accident the previous week.

**CHURCH CHOIRGIRL** Chantelle Bleau, 16, died after sniffing gas lighter fuel at a friend's house. She had a leading role in an anti-drugs play called *Deadly Deals*, which was touring schools in Bradford, West Yorkshire. Chicago schoolgirl Aleia Anderson, 16, took part in a drunk-driving campaign by not speaking to her classmates to show what it would be like if she were no longer there. Then she was killed by a drunken driver. Katrina Taylor, 19, who had impersonated a murder victim in a Crimewatch crime reconstruction, was found stabbed to death in a Brighton churchyard.

**ALL FIVE** members of Brazil's hottest rock band died when their plane crashed into a hill above Guarulhos, their home town, near São Paulo airport. The Mamonas Assassinas (Killer Mammaries) were returning from the final concert of a five-month tour. Last December, São Paulo soothsayer Mother Dinah predicted in the daily *Folha da Tarde* that they would be involved in a plane crash. Hours before the last concert, hair-salon owner Nelson de Lima videotaped keyboard player Julio Rasec as he was having his hair dyed red. "Last night I dreamed something," said Julio on the tape. "It seemed the airplane was falling." As they boarded the plane that night in Brasilia for the flight to Guarulhos, a runway worker wished them luck in their forthcoming overseas debut: "I hope you're a smash in

Portugal." Replied lead singer Dinho Alves: "It's my head I'm going to smash."

**ANDREA RUGA** spent his entire life cursed by his name. He had the same name, birthplace and date of birth as a Mafia god-father accused of a wide range of serious crimes including ter-rorism and kidnapping, and though he led a blameless life working as an ironmonger, police computers couldn't tell the difference. His home was repeatedly raided, at road blocks he was always hauled out of his car for interrogation and at hotels he suffered endless indignities as hysterical staff called the police. In the end it became too much; he pulled into a lay-by near Naples and took a fatal dose of poison. Minutes before he had phoned three senators, three magistrates, a local newspa-per editor and the police chief to say: "I can no longer suffer this double life." Why didn't he just change his name?

**TWO MEN** whose bodies washed ashore in Monmouth County, New Jersey, on 3 April 1997 shared a birthday the fol-lowing day. Robert Wolf of Highlands would have been 24 and Jesse Bostik of Asbury Park would have been 81. Wolf's body was found in Eagles Nest Bay and Bostik about eight miles south. Both apparently drowned.

**OIL EXECUTIVE** Anthony Wilson, 50, left the following instruction in his will: "I specifically request that my remains shall be prepared for burial at sea in traditional naval fashion" and added that £1,000 be provided from his estate to buy champagne to be drunk immediately after his sea burial. In the event, it proved impossible to carry out Wilson's wish. He was killed at sea when the *Maria Alejandra*, a £20 million super-tanker, blew up with him on-board. His body, along with that of his 18-year-old nurse and 34 other people, was never recovered. His son Alistair, 23, said: "We did buy the champagne ... and it was all drunk. There was a memorial service for family and friends and a reception afterwards."

**FRIENDS** of a woman who drowned after being swept into the ocean while posing for photographs were horrified when her body was washed up in front of them when they returned the next day to lay wreaths at the site of her death. The Vietnamese tourist was posing with her back to the sea on rocks near Wollogong, Australia, when the tragedy happened. Extensive helicopter searches by police and lifeguards had failed to locate the corpse after the accident.

**ALBERTO SILVERIA** had just sailed under a bridge in Genoa, Italy, when a tourist leaning over the parapet dropped his camcorder. It hit Alberto on the head and killed him instantly. The horrified holidaymaker escaped charges.

**IN GATESHEAD**, Tyne and Wear, two lamp posts toppled within a week of each other. On the first occasion, the post crashed onto a van being driven by 39-year-old Gordon Mitchell of Newcastle, killing him instantly. The statement made by the police that this was "a million-to-one tragedy" looked a bit premature when 48 hours later, the second post toppled, fortunately without injuring anyone this time. Gateshead council checked out the remaining lamp posts in the area and declared the OK, but could give no explanation as to why the two had collapsed.

**ACTOR** and novelist Roger Bowen, who portrayed Col. Henry Blake in the 1970 film version of *M*A*S*H*, died of a heart attack one day after McLean Stevenson, who portrayed Blake in the TV series, died, also of a heart attack.

CHAPTER THREE

# *Love 'n' Marriage*

**The path of true love is never smooth, and for some it is bumpier than others.**

**CARLOS JIMINEZ** was freed by a court in Coro, Venezuela, after killing his wife Maria when he rolled over in bed and hit her with his elbow.

**A DEVOTED COUPLE**, married for 44 years, died within seconds of each other at their home in Huyton, Merseyside. Margaret Connell, 63, collapsed after seeing her husband Pat, 66, suffer a heart attack. They were childhood sweethearts and left 11 children and 26 grandchildren. Also going together were Catherine Whisker (Cat Whisker?) and her husband Leslie. Mrs Whisker was in a car following the ambulance carrying Leslie to hospital when she turned to her son Paul and said she was feeling unwell; she too collapsed with a heart attack. The couple was admitted to the emergency unit and died within five minutes of each other. The Whiskers had been inseparable since childhood.

**BEATRIZ ROBELDO**, 47, became so annoyed with her husband's hiccups as he was settling down for a nap that she tried to scare him. The plan went horribly wrong. Nestor Lutz, 48, was so shocked when he opened his eyes and saw a figure crouching over him wearing a spooky carnival mask that he grabbed a knife and stabbed his wife to death. He then panicked and threw the body into a septic tank before turning himself in to police. The tragedy happened in the provincial Argentinian town of Ituzaingo on 12 January 1997. Similarly unfortunate was Siek Phan, 62, a Vietnamese woman from the Cambodian province of Kompong Speu, who was cutting firewood when her husband, Nou Meas, 65, sneaked up and tickled her. She instinctively threw her axe, killing him instantly. When she turned round she found she had nearly decapitated him. "I hate being tickled," she told the authorities.

**VERNON SUCKERLOG** (or Suchard or Serlog), 65, from Birmingham, Alabama (or possibly Arkansas), had collected his toenails for 55 (or 40) years and had stored four tons of old clippings in his attic. One night, he was bathing when the ceiling collapsed, showering him with old toenails and killing him instantly. His wife was unsympathetic: "He only married me because I'm a trained pedicurist," said Sally-Anne Suckerlog (or Suchard or Serlog). Do you believe a word of this?

**OR, INDEED, THIS?** According to the *News of the World*, a middle-aged, one-legged Frenchman, interrupted in flagrante, collapsed and died after a one-mile hop to escape a cuckolded husband. Hmm. In Bogota, Colombia, however, Emilio Garcia, 23, jumped naked out of the second-floor window of his mistress' house after her husband arrived home unexpectedly ... and impaled himself on the handlebars of his motorbike. Police said he had apparently forgotten that he had parked the bike below. He died in hospital during an operation to remove the machine from his groin.

**WHEN** Italian two-timer Paolo Fusari's jealous wife shot him, the bullet missed and went into a tree. But it 'fired' and killed him 13 years later when he used explosives to fell the oak. Also jealous was a man aged 100, from Medan in Indonesia, who believed his 75-year-old wife was having an affair. He killed her by cutting her throat after she refused to have sex with him.

**ROCK-CLIMBING LOTHARIO** Claudio Fortunati fell 242 feet to his death from the top of a cliff on the holiday island of Ponza when his safety rope gave way. It had been severed with pliers or a similar tool, though the police were unsure whether by a dumped girlfriend or a jealous boyfriend.

**THIERRY SIGAUD**, 31, shot and killed his mother on 6 September after she gave him a haircut he did not like in preparation for a local carnival in Nevers, France. His father tried to intervene and was also shot dead.

**AN UNNAMED** 25-year-old Argentinian man pushed his wife out of the window of their eighth-floor Buenos Aires apartment. As she fell, she got tangled in power cables. He plummeted to his death when he tried to free her and his wife managed to pull herself up onto a balcony.

**A VIETNAMESE** man who intervened in a row between his married neighbours and pacified them, helped himself to a drink. Unfortunately, the bottle of water had been poisoned by the husband, who had earlier intended committing suicide. He died an hour later.

**ROCK MUSICIAN** David Alexander Richmond, 28, from Sanford, Florida, had been missing for over a year when his former girlfriend Michele Roger, 27, made the mistake of telling friends she had killed him. The topless dancer had stabbed him during an argument. She called her family for help and they took the corpse to a field to burn. They then mulched the skeleton in a Richmond's own tree chipper, mixed the remains with concrete and drove towards Miami on Interstate 95 throwing small chunks out the window as they went.

**KEVIN MURRAY,** 20, from Edinburgh, hanged himself from a 'Way Out' road sign at Wester Hailes railway station after a row with his girlfriend. He was discovered on 7 July 1996.

**CHRISTOPHER** Sean Payne, 34, and an un-named woman of 25 drank 11 bottles of beer on 11 October 1996 and then went on a sexual romp in the sea off Pee Wee Camp beach near Darwin in Australia. They had intercourse in "a number of positions" before the woman went underwater to perform fellatio. Payne became excited, put his hands on her head and kept her submerged. Michael Carey, prosecuting at Payne's trial in the Northern Territories Supreme Court a year later, said Payne told police that when the woman stopped sucking, he wondered what was going on, so he let her up. She had not tried to get up and wasn't kicking or splashing. When he realised she was dead, he 'freaked out', dressed and drove away. He was arrested two days later. During his year in prison, he had constant nightmares and was treated 12 times for outbreaks of boils. Payne's counsel pointed out that the woman might have passed out from drink; she had consumed six times the legal driving limit.

**WHILE** it may not the best idea to have oral sex under water, doing it while driving is possibly even less wise, as Malcolm Whitham, 41, and Susan Charman, 37, found out. When police reached the wreck of their car, which had slammed into a pub at high speed, they found Whitham drunk at the wheel with his trousers and underpants round his knees and Charman, naked from the waist up, draped across his lap. She had died instantly from a broken neck; Whitham died later from multiple injuries. Police sergeant Roy Simpson told the inquest: "It's my view that Mr Whitham's attention was not committed 100 per cent to having control of the vehicle."

**A LUSTFUL ENCOUNTER** also saw off Ralf and Pia Broom, who died during a passionate interlude on a dining-room table; both died when a massive chandelier fell from the ceiling and crushed them. A romantic crush also ended a Zambian couple's erotic episode, this time in a church. They were making love frenziedly when a wall fell on top of them, killing the man and leaving the woman injured beneath him. In Los Angeles, Robert Salazar was arrested after Sandra Orellana, one of his employees, fell to her death from the terrace of her room at the Industry Hills Sheraton Resort and Conference Centre. He had failed to report her death, which occurred as they were making love on the eighth-floor terrace. She toppled over the rail while changing position and crashed to her death 50ft below. Investigating officer Deputy Elsa Mangana said "I can't recall anything like this occurring. It takes your breath away."

**WHEN** Sharon R Lopatka left her home in Hampstead, Maryland, on 13 October, she wrote a note for her husband saying she was going to visit friends in Georgia and would not be coming back. "If my body is never retrieved, don't worry:

know that I'm at peace," she wrote. She also asked him not to go after her attacker. In the event, Lopatka took a 300-mile bus ride to North Carolina, where she expected to be sexually tortured and killed by a man she had corresponded with over the Internet. Apparently, she got her wish. Her body was found in a shallow grave in late October behind a mobile home in Collettsville belonging to Robert Glass, who was charged with first-degree murder. The autopsy showed she had been strangled about 16 October. Messages from Glass, recovered from Lopatka's home computer, indicate that she travelled to North Carolina knowing what awaited her. Lopatka, 35, operated three World Wide Web pages. One offered to write classified advertisements, while the other two, advertising psychic hot lines, were entitled 'Psychics Know All', and 'Dionne Enterprises'. A friend described her as happily married and sensible. Glass, 45, a father of three who separated from his wife earlier that year, had worked as a computer programmer for the county for nearly 16 years. The two first came in contact over the Internet. Lopatka's husband reported her missing on 20 October and police discovered the e-mail messages from Glass, despite his attempt to have her erase the files. Messages from 'Slowhand' – Glass's apparent Internet alias – "described in detail how he was going to sexually torture … and ultimately kill her," an affidavit said.

**SKINHEAD** Adamo Cacchione made fun of his father Egidio by giving him the fascist salute whenever he spoke to him. In the end, Egidio, 63, got fed up with this … and shot Adamo dead. Percy Washington, on the other hand, was full of remorse after trying to shoot his wife. Being short-sighted, he mistook neighbour Fannie Watson for his spouse and shot her dead instead. "It's just a pity for Mrs Watson that I forgot to take my glasses," said Washington, 61.

# *God Have Mercy*

**You would think the devout and the superstitious
would lead a charmed life, but …**

**PASTOR** Michael Davis, of the Larose Christian Fellowship
Church in Louisiana, finished his sermon, stripped down to his
bathing trunks, exhorted the faithful to prepare for rebirth and
stepped into the pool where he intended to baptise a dozen of
his flock. Unfortunately, his microphone was badly grounded;
the resulting explosion left the pastor floating belly up and
melted the microphone.

**FORMER ANGLICAN MINISTER** John Oldland, 88, got
his last wish when he was ordained as a Roman Catholic priest
five minutes before he died of a heart attack. He had a heart
attack just hours before the ceremony was due to take place at
St Anne's Church, Bethnal Green, but survived long enough to
go through with it at the Royal London Hospital, Whitechapel.
In Ireland, Fr Liam Cosgrave, a Roman Catholic priest, died of
a heart attack in a gay sauna and was given last rites there by

two other priests. Staff at the Incognito sauna said Fr Cosgrave was a regular.

**VILJI BHAGAT**, 37, who had a reputation in Gujerat for great piety, climbed into a grave dug for him by his followers. He sat meditating, with a coconut balanced on his head, while his followers buried him alive. His wife then lit Bristol cigarettes to perfume her husband's grave.

**DAVID DOWNING**, 47, of Sheffield, became obsessed with UFOs, aliens and all things paranormal. He took to wandering naked inside and outside his house in the three weeks before his death, which was timed to coincide with a partial eclipse of the sun. On the day of the eclipse, he wrapped electrical cable around himself and plugged himself into the mains. Charts and maps left behind indicated that he thought he would go straight to the afterlife if the sun struck his body correctly.

**AT LEAST** 118 Muslim pilgrims died in a stampede on the last day of the haj at Mina, outside Mecca in Saudi Arabia. Around noon on 9 April 1998, pilgrims were 'stoning the Devil', which involves throwing seven chickpea-sized stones at each of the three pillars at Jamraat on the Mina plain three times over three days. Each pillar symbolises one of the temptations of Satan. Some elderly and ill pilgrims fell off the Jamraat bridge; most deaths occurred in the ensuing rush. An estimated 2.3 million pilgrims from about 100 countries took part in the 1998 haj. On 2 July 1990, 1,426 pilgrims were crushed in a tunnel stampede in Mecca; on 23 May 1994, 270 died in a stampede during the 'stoning the Devil' ritual; and on 15 April 1997, 343 pilgrims died when a fire swept through 70,000 tents.

**STAMPEDES** are not the exclusive property of the Muslim community – other religions manage quite well too. Fifty-eight people died and at least 100 were injured in stampedes at two Hindu shrines involving worshippers who gathered to pray for protection on 15 July 1996, an unlucky day, according to astrologers. About 35 of the fatalities occurred at the Siva temple complex in Ujjain in the central state of Madhya Pradesh. Some of the victims were crushed, others impaled on a bamboo barricade. The annual pilgrimage to the Amarnath Cave, 12,725ft up in the Kashmir Mountains, claimed at least 214 lives in August 1996 because of heavy snow and rain, landslides and freezing temperatures. Some 112,000 Hindus came to Kashmir for the 1996 pilgrimage to the cave's ice stalagmite, which is regarded as a lingam (phallus) of the god Siva.

**TWENTY-NINE** died on 11 January 1998 in the flood-swollen and crocodile-infested Limpopo River bordering Zimbabwe and South Africa. A preacher of the Apostolic Faith sect had knelt on the river bank in prayer and said that he had received 'divine guidance' that God had cleared the way for them. Three days later, the death toll from trying to cross the Limpopo had risen to 36. In 1995 thousands turned out to watch a Zairian preacher prove that he could walk on water like Christ. The audience watched in horror as he was swept away by the strong currents of the River Kwipu, from which his body was recovered three days later.

**FORTUNE TELLER** Patrick Depalle was supremely confident when he played Russian roulette to impress a customer who doubted his mystic powers: "My spirit contacts on the other side will protect me," he said before pulling the trigger. His last words before blowing his brains out were: "I never make a mistake." In Britain, astrologer Patrick Walker died on

8 October 1995, but was still publishing his predictions in the *Newcastle Evening Chronicle* on Friday 13 October.

**TWO MUSLIMS** in western Nigeria went to offer special prayers at Sobi Hill after the Eid-al-Adha feast at the weekend of 27–28 April. A storm broke out and in a spectacular display of divine ingratitude, the two men were struck dead by lightning and four others knocked unconscious. A mob killed Jim Motloutsi, 73, in the village of Mmatobole in Northern Province, South Africa. They stoned him, doused him with petrol, placed a tyre round his neck and set him alight. They held him responsible for the death of a 60-year-old woman who had been killed by lightning in the village a few days earlier.

**TURKISH** barman Oguz Atak appeared on the Islamic television station TGRT on 4 May with the word 'Allah' tattooed in Arabic on his shoulder and was accused of "making fun of religion." Two hit-men from an ultra-nationalist group who had seen the programme shot him dead the next day and were arrested soon after. "We were deeply enraged," they said. "He had to pay."

**FOUR FILIPINO** teenagers belonging to the Pentecost International Christian Community, a cult that predicted the world would end on New Year's Day 1996, strangled their mother on 3 January after the prophecy proved wrong. They believed she was possessed by the devil. The woman was found dead in her home in Luyao village, 165 miles north of Manila. At least 30 members of the cult had locked themselves in a compound on 28 December to await Judgment Day, but they were persuaded to abandon their vigil on 2 January.

IN ANNAPOLIS, Maryland, Michael W Turner was sentenced to 30 years in prison for bludgeoning his mother to death with a statue of the Virgin Mary. Police found Marie Turner's corpse in her bedroom with the bloody statue beside her. They believed Turner had killed her during an argument after he borrowed her car without permission.

THE REV'D Adrienne Simondson, one of Australia's first women priests, died in a freak accident in South Africa. The bus she and a group of girls were taking to Victoria Falls broke down and Rev'd Simondson volunteered to fetch spare parts. Her vehicle collided with an elephant and she died instantly.

A HOME-MADE rocket aimed at the heavens during a temple rocket festival in Chantaburi province, Thailand, on 1 June nose-dived, hitting village headman Chom Inchan, 48, on the head and killing him instantly. He was among hundreds of villagers gathered at the annual Bun Bang fire festival when bamboo or iron tube rockets are launched during planting to ask the gods to water the crops.

A NEW ZEALAND health authority was sued by the family of Monty Winikirei, who died in hospital in 1995. They claimed that the hospital broke a Maori taboo that a body must be buried whole by not telling the family that his amputated legs were not in the coffin.

GREEN PARTY activist Nicholas Galgani, 26, who believed himself the victim of a witches' coven, was found dead from multiple injuries at the base of a 300ft cliff near his home in Lewes, East Sussex. He had been trying out some 'magical practices' and had been sent a voodoo doll and a cow's heart hammered through with nails shortly before his death, an inquest at Brighton was told on 12 June 1996. He had told his girlfriend that he was having nightmares about a 'black apparition'. When detectives went to his flat, they discovered black crosses daubed across the doors and painted on the wall in foot-high letters the plea: "Please God. Somebody save me. Protect me from black magic." Pages from a Bible had also been pasted on the wall. The police inquiry into Galgani's death was also examining a number of "unusual happenings" in Lewes, according to Detective Sergeant Bates, who said: "In recent weeks, graves have been desecrated and cats killed and nailed to posts outside churches. In the latest incident [on 11 June], three graves were desecrated."

**IN BOGOTA**, Colombia, Rev Jesus David Saenz and a woman parishioner, Marina Rojas, died after drinking cyanide-laced wine which had been sent to the priest as an Easter gift. Police warned that a Satanic cult might be behind the poisoning after 12 churches received poisoned wine in the mail. Rev Ricardo Martinez, head of one of the churches which also received poisoned wine, claimed that "Satan-worshippers were preparing human sacrifices for Easter."

# *That's Entertainment, or At Least It Was*

**The entertainment world is fraught with hidden dangers … but nothing is as entertaining as a surreal demise.**

**FOUR SKYDIVING** Elvis impersonators were blown off-course while trying to land in the car park of the WaterWorks nightclub in Marina Bay, Boston, USA; one was killed during its opening celebrations. With a fine ear for a memorable phrase, John McNulty of the Boston police said: "Elvis hit town – he just hit it a bit too hard."

**JULIAN POWELL**, 33, collapsed and died after riding on the aptly-named Nemesis roller coaster at Alton Towers theme park, Staffordshire. Elsewhere, a 17-year-old Hong Kong girl was killed when a tethered balloon she was strapped to broke free and drifted 25 miles before bursting and throwing her to the ground. The body of the teenager, part of a tour group visiting a movie theme park in Panyu, southern China, was found five hours after the balloon took off.

**ALSO** falling foul of a balloon was children's entertainer Marlon Pistol, who was killed when a 20ft balloon elephant used in his act started to inflate in the back of his car on a California highway.

**DANCER** James Saunders, 50, fell 30ft to his death while performing a handstand on a staircase railing outside the Ludwig Museum in Cologne. More than 500 people were watching the solo performance when Saunders misjudged his spring and crashed to his death. He had performed the handstand before, but the second time sprang onto the railing with too much force.

**EXOTIC DANCER** Lucia La Bella launched a new nightclub act during which she whirled a pistol, but during her performance the gun went off and customer Mario Rosinni, 50, dropped dead. When charged with reckless endangerment, Lucia pleaded that she did not know the gun was loaded.

**STAG PARTY** friends were curious when a stripper failed to jump out of a huge cake in Cosenza, Italy. Then they found her dead inside it. Gina Lalapola, 23, had suffocated after waiting for an hour inside the sealed cake.

**DAREDEVIL** Bobby Leach was one of the few people to survive going over Niagara Falls in a barrel. In 1911, he made the 168ft plunge in front of a 30,000-strong audience and was pulled out unconscious but alive. Twenty-five years later, he slipped on a piece of orange peel in Auckland, New Zealand ... and died in hospital after having his leg amputated as a result of the injuries suffered. In Sydney, Australia, Robbie Hanifer, also described as 'a daredevil', didn't have to wait 25 years; his attempt to win £1,000 by diving 30ft into a pile of horse manure failed badly; he missed the pile and died after hitting the ground.

**COMEDY SHOW** *Make 'em Laugh*, scheduled to open at Leeds City Varieties Theatre on Friday 13 September 1996, was cancelled after two of its star comedians died. In London, however, they kill the audience rather than the stars. Mark Anthony, 28, a life assurance consultant, went to see Lee Hurst's show at the Up the Creek! comedy club in Greenwich. Ten minutes after the start of the show, he laughed so hard that he choked to death. Danny La Rue pulled the same stunt at the Playhouse in Weston-super-Mare. Attending the drag artist's *Danny Goes to Hollywood* show for the second time, 78-year-old Greta Warburton laughed so hard in her front row seat that she gave herself a stroke. Rushed to hospital, she died seven hours later. "It's what she would have chosen," a friend said.

**A CIRCUS TRAINER'S** shiny new suit may have caused a Bengal tiger to attack him during a performance. Wayne Franzen, 50, founder of the Franzen Brothers' Circus, died within minutes after suffering a punctured lung and neck wounds before an audience of 200 children and their families at Broad Top City, Carrolltown, Pennsylvania. The 400lb tiger, one of three in the cage, attacked Franzen when he turned his back, then dragged him around the ring by his neck. The circus, which began in 1974, was one of the most respected of America's 'mud shows'.

**PATIENTS** and employees of a Corpus Christi, Texas, physical therapy centre thought that William Chadwick, 31, was a realistic hanged man at a haunted house party. Then they noticed that the ropes had slipped and really strangled him. The same happened to an un-named 41-year-old Cambridge,

Massachusetts, man at a Hallowe'en party in 1988. And to 15-year-old William Odom from York, South Carolina, at another Hallowe'en party in 1990. For Brian Jewell, 17, of Lakewood, New Jersey, death came during his after-school job at the Hangman's Scene attraction run by Haunted Hayrides Inc. The organisers spotted that all was not well when Jewell failed to deliver his spooky speech. In another eerie attraction, the dungeon of a ruined 13th-century castle in Slovenska Lupca, central Slovakia, an actor simulating a hanged man accidentally hanged himself too. No-one noticed that the 33-year-old man, who had tested the procedure several times, was dead until tourists pushed his body in fun as it dangled from the rope.

**ALSO** leaving the audience in suspense was a British actor who hanged himself while playing Judas during an open-air performance of *Jesus Christ Superstar* in front of an audience of 600 holidaymakers at a Greek hotel. Tony Wheeler, 26, failed to attach the rope to a hook on his back designed to support his weight. He remained hanging above a small rise at the dimly-lit side of the stage for about six minutes before the actors and audience realised that his initial spasms were more than realistic acting. Several doctors in the audience at the Sani Beach Hotel at Kassandra on the northern Greek peninsula of Chalkidiki tried unsucessfully to revive Mr Wheeler.

**RICHARD VERSALLE**, 63, died when he fell 10ft from a ladder on to the stage of the Metropolitan Opera House in New York on 5 January during the opening scene of *The Makropulos Case*, Janáček's opera about the secret of eternal life. It was thought that he had suffered a heart attack. Versalle, who was alone on stage, was portraying a law clerk named Vitek, who has climbed a ladder to return papers a filing cabinet. The last line he sang, in the English translation of the original Czech, was "Too bad you can only live so long," a reference to a protracted lawsuit that was finally about to be settled. Versalle fell, landing on his back with his arms outstretched. The curtain was swiftly lowered and he was rushed to hospital, but was dead on arrival.

**SOCIOLOGISTS** in the U.S. think they have found a link between the number of times country music is played on the radio and the suicide rate among urban white males in parts of America. "This effect was independent of variations in gun ownership, divorce rate or poverty," they said. They claimed to be able to demonstrate a link between country music, with themes such as heavy alcohol consumption and depression, and used it to predict suicide rates. Another group also claimed they could predict economic recession by analysing the pessimism of lyrics in the pop charts.

**CANADIAN ACTOR** Jonathan Hartman, 39, whose attempts to join the Royal Shakespeare Company were continually spurned, worked out a sure-fire way to perform with them. He left them his skull so that he could play Hamlet's dead jester, Yorick, for eternity. A codicil of his will states: "Because of my love of classical theatre and especially the works of William Shakespeare, I have decided, given the transitory nature of employment so common in to my profession, to ensure myself a ... perpetual, posthumous engagement." Elaborating on this he said: "I may not know what my next job will be, but I want to ensure I know what my last job will be." The Royal Shakespeare Company, however, seemed determined to thwart Hartman to the end. Zoë Mylchreest said: "We couldn't use a real skull on stage, as bone is too brittle and the skulls get some rough handling."

**JACK NANCE**, 53, who played Henry, the nightmare-ridden bachelor with the electrified bouffant hairdo in David Lynch's surreal horror film *Eraserhead* (1977), exited in an a fittingly strange manner: he died shortly after being hit on the head in an argument in his local doughnut shop. Joining him in the appropriate exit stakes were further media folk. Richard Niquette, host of the *Murder and Mystery* programme on a Canadian interactive TV channel, died on the street outside his Montreal home after being repeatedly stabbed in the heart, while Hollywood director Al Adamson, 66, who specialised in low-budget slasher films such as *Five Bloody Graves* and *Horror of the Blood Monster*, was found murdered and buried under a jacuzzi in his desert home at Indio, 150 miles from Los Angeles.

**SHOWBIZ AGENT** Atal Bakht could still have got any of them a movie role though, if not a starring one. Atal buys corpses from families in India who cannot afford to give their relatives a proper send-off, then has them embalmed by a specialist and rents them out as extras for crowd scenes in the thriving Bombay film industry. "The dead give me a good living," said Atal. "They always look good, they never complain, and there are no pay cheques at the end of the month." He also had plans to branch out into the security business, reckoning that he could make a killing hiring out uniformed stiffs to banks.

# CHAPTER SIX

# *Homes and Gardens*

**Most people see their homes as a refuge, but more accidents happen there than anywhere else.**

**A COUPLE** in Hamburg were trapped when the door of their home-made sauna jammed and the temperature soared to 180°. As lawyer Sigrid Wildberg, 53, hammered on the door and screamed for help, husband Achsen, 60, tried to wrench off the pine roofing. Then, overcome by the heat, he died. Sigrid passed out as she ripped wiring off a wall, but she had caused a short circuit which cut off the heating. She was rescued the next day by a neighbour.

**JOAN DAVIES**, 72, of Little Chalfont, Buckinghamshire, died after slipping in her bathroom and impaling herself on the loo brush. It went straight through her eye and 7in of it entered her brain. It is not known if she died instantly. Her body was found after worried neighbours telephoned police.

**HANS PENDER**, from Salzburg, Austria, suffocated when he got entangled in 60ft of thick wallpaper and couldn't struggle free. "The more he struggled, the tighter the paper wrapped him up," said detective Peter Dieker.

**WEE SEI HENG**, 18 months, was playing in the living room of his family's flat on 6 January 1996 when his mother heard a loud crash and found her son on the floor, bleeding from nose and mouth, next to their 30kg television with a 29in screen. The boy died two hours later from a fractured skull. He had apparently tried to climb on the set, which was on a display stand.

**IN POLAND**, Czeslaw B, 60, who was so afraid of burglars that he filled his house with deadly booby traps, fell victim to his own safeguards. He was found shot dead outside his garage, killed, according to initial investigations, by two home-made guns mounted on the garage doors. Explosives experts, moving cautiously through his house in Kosianka Trojanowka village, found eight similar traps by the front door, in rooms and in the attic, each device fitted with a discreet off-switch, and 28 more booby traps in the house in various stages of construction. In Bucharest, Romania, Florian Iorga, 42, and his son Aurel, 16, made the same mistake. They were electrocuted by a booby trap they had set up to protect their onion patch. Hearing noises in the night, they ran out to investigate … and tripped over the cables wired to the mains. The bodies were found by the man's wife. The same fate also befell a 49-year-old man in Slatina, Croatia, after he wired up his house and its perimeter against burglars. In Failand, near Bristol, George Hunt, groundsman at the Old Bristolians Rugby Club, was electrocuted as he tried to lure worms to the surface with a live cable tied to a garden fork. Hunt, 48, hoped to catch the worms to use as bait for moles which were damaging the field.

**MARK ROCKINGHAM**, 12, died when he fell on a knife that had been stacked with its blade pointing upwards in the cutlery basket of an open dishwasher. He is believed to have been reaching into a cupboard at his home in Kettering, Northamptonshire, when he lost his balance and fell forwards across the front of the machine. The knife sliced through an artery in his chest and he died in hospital. Elsewhere, David Jenkins, 70, overbalanced while cutting the hedge behind his Brigg, South Humberside, house. He fell backwards off his ladder and lost control of his power hedge trimmer, which almost severed his head.

**TEENAGER** Tanya Nickens was sucked to death by a hot-tub which went out of control. After a dip in an unheated swimming pool, the 16-year-old New Jersey girl joined nine friends in a hot-tub to warm up, but as she submerged herself, she was sucked down by her buttocks into the grate at the bottom of the tub. Her bottom completely covered the grate, making it impossible for rescuers to prise her free: the combined efforts of a lifeguard, a policeman and six friends could not pull her loose. Despite efforts to keep her alive by breathing air into her mouth underwater, she drowned before she could be released. In Kuwait City, a boy aged four drowned in a washing machine after falling in while trying to rescue a ball, and in Germany, Heinz Schmidt, 41, drowned when he tried to retrieve the wallet he had dropped down a toilet in Essen.

**DRUNKEN FARMER** Clifford Greenwood, 67, from Wharfdale, North Yorkshire, drowned on his front room carpet. Stubborn to the last, he refused to leave his home as the swollen river Wharf rapidly swamped his home. As his house filled with water, he sat unruffled in a lawn chair in the front room, wearing a flat cap, sipping whiskey and watching TV, his feet propped up on a brick. When his son's girlfriend Moira Clough phoned and asked if he was drunk, he replied: "I am that, lass," and still refused to leave. She assumed he'd find his way up to bed, but the next morning he was found dead. He'd toppled out of the chair and drowned in the 18 inches of water slopping round his living room.

**A LANDLORD** with "a very limited interest in personal hygiene" died when his three lodgers decided to give him a bath because he was "dirty and smelly." Raymond Davies, 52, was frog-marched to his bathroom, undressed and plunged into a bath of cold water. The shock killed him. Davies and his three lodgers were all heavy drinkers and their home was filthy and unkempt. After Davies died, his lodgers left him for six days and carried on drinking.

**A COLLECTOR** whose house was so full of junk he could not use the front door died after becoming stuck trying to climb through an upstairs window. David Ellis, in his sixties, was found by fire-fighters with his legs sticking out of the window at his home in Handsworth, Birmingham. In Bradford, West Yorkshire, police found Michael McNamara, 37, pinned at the waist in a six-inch gap between a wooden door and its frame in a second-floor flat. He had become trapped when a piece of wood fell behind the door, jamming it almost shut, and died within half an hour of his release. He had broken into the empty flat and had been stuck in the doorway for two days. An 87-year-old man in Setubal, Portugal, who always left and entered his second-floor flat by climbing a rope, died when it broke.

**THE BROOKLYN UNION** Gas Company tried for months to gain entrance to a house in 110th Street, Forest Hills,

Queens, to read the meter. On 1 December 1994, workers arrived with a locksmith and a city marshal. They entered the basement, where they found a corpse behind a huge cobweb, seated on a patio chair near the boiler. The deceased was identified as Long Lu Lee, 69, a retired mechanical engineer. He was wearing a blue bathrobe, white sweater, jogging trousers, white socks and sandals. His head had dropped off and was found beneath the chair. His widow Thuc Khoanh Lu, 62, told police that her husband had disappeared the previous winter, but that she had never filed a missing person report – she seemed genuinely surprised to learn that he had been dead in her basement all year and was not considered a suspect in his death.

**WHEN** she was six, Rolande Genève planted an oak in her garden in Isère, France. Sixty years later, it fell over and killed her.

**ANDREW THORNTON**, 37, received a fatal shock as he turned on the shower at his home in Banbury, Oxfordshire. A small screw used to tighten a loose floorboard on the landing outside the bathroom had penetrated wiring for the shower and caused a short circuit. In Louisiana, a man building a backyard swing was electrocuted when sweat dripped into a power drill he was using.

**A MAN** fell 200ft to his death when his ride-on lawnmower went over a cliff. Ken Campbell, 55, had been cutting the grass at his holiday home at Port Angeles, near Seattle. He turned sharply to avoid the cliff edge, but the mower, locked in high gear, rolled over and tumbled down a sandstone bluff.

**GOOD NEIGHBOURLINESS** can be stretched so far, but then it snaps. In New Orleans, Melvin Hitchens, 66, a man who had a running feud with his neighbours about yard work, finally reached breaking point in 1996. He picked up his gun, killed a woman as she swept the sidewalk and then injured her husband as he mowed the lawn. In Japan, a man's bid to beat the world record for non-stop drumming failed when a fed-up neighbour burst in and knifed him to death, and in Bowling Green, Ohio, university freshman Julia Miller, 22, ended up in court after she threatened to shoot her room-mate's compact disc player. It was a "bit of an annoyance to her," campus official Barbara Waddell explained.

**JOHN VANDERSTAM**, 47, also got upset about noise. The Birmingham man killed himself after "going through hell" when noisy neighbours moved in next door to the house he shared with his father, Adrian, 78. At his inquest, the coroner stated that noise had been "a cogent factor" in his death. It was vegetables which got to Asa Denny, 68. He killed himself when his huge tomato failed to win the top prize at a country fair in Grafton, Australia.

# Misjudging Machines

**Tangling with technology is never wise –
and sometimes it's fatal.**

**WELFARE CLERK** James Chenault, 54, boarded a lift in the Kingsbridge Welfare Center in the Bronx with four other people. It raced up to the second floor, apparently out of control. When the doors opened, Chenault straddled the doorway to allow the others off. One made it out, but with the doors still open, the lift resumed its climb, decapitating Chenault. His head, wearing stereo headphones, fell into the lift with the three remaining passengers and his body fell down the shaft.

**EMMA NISKALA**, 35, was crushed to death in what the police described as "about as freak an accident as you can imagine." She walked onto an escalator at a New York office and travelled for a few feet before the step she was standing on gave way. She was swallowed by the mechanism and efforts to pull her out failed. Earlier in the year, a Washington man was strangled by a subway escalator. It was thought that he had been lying on the escalator at the time of his death.

**LISA POTTER**, 21, went for a walk at night with her mother, Mrs Ann Everitt of Witham. They came to the Moots Lane railway crossing where Lisa's father had been killed 11 years earlier, and Mrs Everitt refused to continue. Lisa went and stood on the track and called, "Come on, Mum, it's alright." At that moment, a train light appeared and Lisa was run over and killed. Vittorio Verroni was killed on the Via Cartoccio level crossing in Reggio Emilia, northern Italy, when his Renault 21 was hit by a train and carried along the line. The crossing, over the Guastella-Reggio line – unmanned and without any protective bar, the legal norm for Italy's local railways – was near a bend in a flat landscape and the morning sun can be dangerously blinding. Signor Veroni's daughter Cristina, 19, had been killed four years earlier, on 19 January 1991, another sunny morning, at the same crossing, by the same train, driven by the same driver. Signor Veroni, 57, a builder from nearby Novellara, drove back and forth to work several times a day over the crossing. Suggestions that he decided to take his life at the place where his daughter died were repudiated by his family and the train driver, Domenico Serafino. Investigators said his death was accidental. They believed that he was either blinded by the sun or was hindered from turning to look before crossing because of a plaster cast he wore around his chest following a workplace accident.

**HERMAN LORENZ**, 88, was knocked down and killed by a train at a crossing in the Chicago suburb of Northbrook. Witnesses said he went round the crossing gates and kept going after the Amtrak train engineer sounded a warning horn. In October 1926, Lorenz survived a crash at the same crossing. A train sliced through the school bus he was riding, killing two people, including his seatmate.

**AN UNNAMED** 24-year-old Garfield, New Jersey, man was found dead under the wheels of his car in November 1994. It appeared that he had been drinking before he got into the car and started the ignition. He leant out of the car to vomit but instead of leaving the car in neutral, he put it into reverse. When he fell out, taking his foot off the brake, the car ran over his head and neck.

**MILIKA SLOAN**, soaking wet and barefoot, swiped her electronic key card through the steel lock of her hotel door and fried. A power surge from a faulty air-conditioning unit killed the 18-year-old Cincinnati woman, who was attending an employment training programme in Maryland.

**PAUL BROWNRIGG**, 16, from Littlehampton, West Sussex, had twice the legal driving limit of alcohol in his blood when he boasted to friends that he could lick the live rail on a railway line near his home. As he leant towards the line a spark leapt from the 750-volt rail, crisping him instantly.

**A 27-YEAR-OLD** French woman, driving near Marseilles, killed a cyclist and injured another when she was distracted by distress signals from the Tamagotchi attached to her car keyring. She asked a passenger to attend to the electronic ovoid; in the confusion, she failed to see a group of cyclists on the road ahead and slammed into the back of them. The popular Japanese toys send out electronic bleeps when they need 'feeding' or 'cleaning'. If they are not looked after, they 'die'.

**HECTOR PENNA** spent four years developing a powerful factory cooling fan. He was modifying his invention in his laboratory in San Julian, Argentina, when his wife walked in and flicked on the light switch, not realising he had connected it to the fan. He was decapitated by the blades.

**A TEENAGER** who spent two months in a coma after she was knocked down by a car in November 1989 in the Grampian village of Whitecairns was killed on 22 February when she was hit by a lorry at the same spot. Both accidents occurred when Gillian Sylvester, 19, crossed a main road to a bus stop opposite her house.

**HELGA FISCHER**, 29, went into hospital for a minor operation in Bonn, Germany. She was slightly worried, so her husband Herbert decided to cheer her up. An experienced pilot, the 31-year-old teacher hired a Cessna 150 and flew it towards the hospital towing a canvas banner with "Get well soon, Helga" painted on it. He swooped to roof height and began circling the building and Helga, seeing him fly past, smiled and waved back, but her smile curdled as she saw the Cessna clip a treetop, lose height and slam into the ground. Herbert was killed instantly and Helga ended up in intensive care suffering from deep shock.

**THE BODY** of a young man, 18-25 years old, was found floating in the Harbour Isle Marina in Island Park, Long Island, in the flight path to Kennedy Airport, on 21 May. A homeowner reported hearing a loud boom, then a splash, at 3.25pm. The victim carried Dominican currency and wore jeans that were not manufactured in the U.S. An American Airlines jet landed at Kennedy just three minutes after the splash and would have been at 2000ft, lowering its landing gear, at the time. Two days later, at 6.35am, a boy cycling to school found a mangled body in the middle of a suburban street about 8.5 miles west-south-west of Miami International Airport. Neighbours heard a thump, but had not investigated. The body was covered in grease stains, suggesting that the man had been a stowaway in the well of an airliner. A third dead stowaway was found in Brooklyn in the hold of a ship that arrived from the Dominican Republic with a load of raw sugar. The body was aboard the MV *Capo Falcone*, which had docked in the Domino refinery in Greenpoint.

**A POLICE OFFICER** at Cairo's main station noticed blood running down the side of a train 22 February and discovered a human head on the roof. The rest of the body was found 60 miles away, on the ground near the bridge which had decapitated Mohamed Zaher Abderrahman, 22, in the Nile delta town of Kafr al-Zayyat.

**A MAN** whose wife had been killed in January 1994 when her snowmobile was hit by a car was fatally injured when his snowmobile ran into a barbed wire fence. Michael Staring, 35, of Pulaski, NY, died on 18 February after the accident in Lewis, about 45 miles northeast of Syracuse. The glare of the sun off the snow apparently caused him to misjudge the distance between the fence and an open gate.

**PENSIONER** Alfredo Cornia from Bologna was killed by a valve radio he'd had since 1941 when it blew up on him. A police spokesman said, "He was a bit deaf and always put his ear to the radio, so when it blew up he was killed outright."

**IN AN EFFORT** to kill fish, Daniel Wyman, 29, and his friend tossed an M-250 firecracker into Fox Lake, Illinois. A gust of wind pushed their 14ft (4m) aluminium rowing boat over the firecracker, which holed the vessel and sank it 300ft (90m) from the shore. Wyman drowned while his friend swam to safety.

**A 49-YEAR-OLD ACCOUNTANT** in St Louis pried open an oft-stuck lift door with a rod, squeezed through and fell to her death. The elevator indicator was correctly showing that the car was one floor above.

**A NEWBORN** baby in a Chicago hospital came to an abrupt end when someone accidentally connected the child's heart monitor cables attached to electrodes on the chest and abdomen directly to the mains. Twelve-day-old Stratton Vasilakos died instantly. Apparently this was caused by a design fault which had resulted in several previous incidents, but was supposed to have been corrected.

**A COUPLE** who got off on the danger of making love on a railway line were killed when the train came before they did. The pair, in their twenties, got so excited that they failed to hear the goods train approaching and were sliced to pieces when it rolled straight over them. Police in Arad, Romania, said "They loved to finish sex before the train arrived, this time they were too late."

# *Beginnings, Middles and Ends*

**Life is traditionally punctuated by three great events, birth, marriage and death; but even in the midst of life there is death – and, in fact, even in the midst of death, there's more death.**

**SMARTARSE** Charles DeLonde of Port au Prince, Haiti, got more than he bargained for when he mocked the institution of marriage. Driving past a church where a wedding was taking place, he hung out of his car and yelled "SUCKER!!" at the groom. But while doing so he lost control of his vehicle, swerved across the road and was killed instantly in a head-on smash with another car.

**A GUEST** at a wedding near Omdurman in the Sudan fell off his camel while firing his AK-47 assault rifle in the air in celebration and accidentally hosed the crowd with high-powered bullets, killing three people. A similar trick was pulled by a Turk in Copenhagen celebrating a Christmas Eve wedding by shooting into the air. The 36-year-old man killed two guests and wounded nine when his 12 shots bounced off a concrete ceiling. He was charged with manslaughter. Going tooled up to a wedding seems to be a recipe for disaster; two more wedding guests died in a gun battle in Aswan, Egypt, after the bride offended family honour by holding her husband's hand, breaking an ancient custom of not showing affection in public.

**IN SOUTHERN IRAN** exuberant merry-making at one wedding led to unforeseen tragedy. The father and sister of the bridegroom got so excited that they dropped dead of heart attacks. It happens in Cardiff too. Bridegroom Joseph Jones, 70, was horrified when his bride, Beryl Howard, 67, slumped to the floor while family and friends sang the first hymn in the marriage service. A nurse and a former ambulanceman in the congregation worked desperately to revive her, but the massive heart attack killed her moments before she was due to say "I do." Still, she got further than Belinda Street, who was walking down the aisle in Adelaide, Australia, when she tripped on her flowing gown, fell, and died of a broken neck.

**NOT EVEN** making it to the church was a Romanian woman, Florica Ifrimie, who hanged herself before her wedding because she could not agree with her bridegroom over the menu for the wedding feast.

**THE BEREAVED PARTNERS** could have taken a leaf out of Feng Lee's book however. Lee was heartbroken when her fiancé died in a tractor accident in China, but this did not deflect her from her determination to wed him; at the ceremony she was ritually joined to a three-foot-high red vase containing his ashes.

**IN FINLAND** Helga Shenkov, 47, refused to let the death of her second husband get in the way of happiness. She claimed what is probably a world record by burying him at 11am, then marrying her third husband at 11.45am.

**IT WASN'T** the death of her partner which ended Francesca Trito's marriage: it was the death of other people's. She divorced her husband after learning that he stole all his clothes from bodies buried in a cemetery close to their home in Spain.

**RECOVERING** from an amputation, Melanie Roberts, 41, from Providence, Ohio, was shocked to receive a bill for $600 for the funeral of her left leg. She was told the leg had been buried and she had to pay for it. The bill was helpfully broken down, providing separate costs for the plot, gravediggers, minister and hearse. She hadn't even been invited to the funeral.

**A JEHOVAH'S WITNESS** who died after refusing a blood transfusion was denied a funeral by church elders. The family of Eira Younger, 64, of Leeds, was told that she had not worshipped often enough.

**A GRAVEDIGGER** died during a funeral at Rookwood Cemetery, Lidcombe, near Sydney, Australia. The 57-year-old man collapsed after widening a grave. "He dug it bigger and we all appreciated that and we were grateful, and then he walked away," said one of the mourners. "He tripped over his shovel and hit his head on a gravestone." This triggered a massive heart attack and although ambulance officers tried six times to revive the man, they were unsuccessful. William Daborn, of Sandhurst, Berkshire, had a heart attack and fell into an open grave at the cemetery where he worked. His body was found by a fellow worker and had to be removed quickly before the grave's intended occupant arrived.

**FRENCH** undertaker Claude Pommereau was killed when a coffin crushed him in his hearse and, with a fine touch, was buried in the box that crushed him.

**AFTER** Vo Lieu, 74, died of natural causes in Vietnam, his children administered a drug to his wife to prevent her screaming at the funeral; but she died of a drug overdose before the ceremony took place. A joint funeral was then held, but a truck transporting the coffins careered out of control and crashed into the procession, killing a 26-year-old man and injuring six undertakers.

**IN MEXICO** driver Francisco Sandoval died in a crash on a fast bend in Santa Cruz. During his funeral two weeks later, the hearse carrying his corpse crashed at the same spot.

**A WEEK BEFORE** she was due to give birth, Wendy Yates, 22, went to her grandmother's funeral. She was at her parents' home in Kings Lynn, Norfolk, when the hearse arrived, but collapsed when she caught sight of it. Thinking she had merely fainted, the rest of the mourners continued to the funeral of Violet Yates, 77, leaving Wendy with her sister Kelly, 16, and an off-duty nurse, Diane Blyth, who called an ambulance. When they arrived they found she had not fainted, but had suffered from a huge rupture of her aorta, and she died before reaching hospital. The shock of seeing the hearse seems to have brought on the fatal hæmorrhage.

**SHOCK** of a different kind killed Claudia Sassi, 57, who collapsed and died at her husband's funeral. Jacques de Putron, a ventriloquist friend of her late husband, later explained that he thought that the mourners would be cheered by a cry of "Let me out!" from the coffin. Police in Lyons, France, noted that throwing one's voice was not against the law.

**EVERY DAY**, Mohammad Saeed Shafiq, 40, visited the grave of his parents in Cairo, where he would weep for hours non-stop. Finally, he cried himself to death at their graveside, according to *Al-Akhbar*, the government daily.

**AN UNSEEMLY** family scrap over a woman's ashes ended up being settled in a Newcastle courtroom. In a will written in 1982, Winnie Johnson stated she wanted her ashes kept and mixed with her husband Alan's when he died. But by the time she died in 1996, she no longer loved him, claimed their daughter Catherine. She persuaded Alan to hand the ashes over to her when she discovered he was ready to flush them down the toilet, but he later demanded their return and, when she refused, took her to court. Judge Esmund Faulkes hammered out a deal where the ashes were kept by a solicitor, and both sides were allowed supervised visits. Mrs Johnson's ashes attended the hearing in an urn contained in a black satchel.

**DEBBIE MENTA**, 32, and Doug Painter, 23, children of the San Diego Chargers quarterback coach Dwain Painter, stood on a high rock above the sea near Mendocino, California, on 2 February 1995, to scatter the ashes of their mother, who had committed suicide the previous month. They were swept into the sea by a powerful wave; Debbie was drowned while her brother struggled to safety.

**WIDOW** Jean Carberry managed to throw her husband Dennis's ashes out with the rubbish and was set to join a search rummaging through the dump to recover them. "I'd know him anywhere," she said. "He was in a green Barnardo's plastic bag." She normally kept the urn in a tub of flowers on her doorstep, but took it in because of rain and put it in a bag to stop it dripping, then she took 30 carriers of rubbish out to the bin and accidentally included the urn. By the time she realised, Dennis was landfill. Council officials said there was only a slim chance of finding him. James Proctor was luckier. His remains resurfaced after seven years – in the spare tyre well of a 1988 Chevy Celebrity. A relative picked up Proctor's ashes after his cremation and put them in the car trunk, but they slipped down into the well and could not be found. Several owners later New Brunswick Auto Exchange discovered the plastic bag with Proctor's remains in and used a metal tag on them to trace their owner.

OVER 20 unburied bodies were found in the shuttered funeral home of Finlay Carter Jnr in Fort Myers, Florida, after the company was evicted for late rent and its business licence revoked. The remains included the skeletons of three infants and a further infant mummified and stuffed in a briefcase. Nine further decomposing corpses were found in a rented storage shed. In Madrid, another negligent undertaker was sued by the widow of a 6ft 7in man after she discovered they'd sawn her husband's legs off to get him in the coffin. In Iceland, the undertaker was forced to flee when grieving relatives discovered their grandfather's corpse had been dressed in a Santa Claus suit for a Christmas funeral, while in Nice, an undertaker had to pay damages to a family after leaving an alarm clock in their grandmother's coffin which went off during the funeral.

HOUSEWIFE Fran Brecht left a will instructing her solicitors in Vienna to ensure she was laid to rest in a crypt alongside her cooker, washing machine and dishwasher. In Stevenage, the NatWest bank was saddled with the unusual funerary stipulations of an 18th-century grocer. When the place re-opened after a hi-tech refit, it still had the coffin of Henry Trigg lodged in the rafters; his will stipulated that his remains be left in the building's rafters as protection against grave robbers.

**ANOTHER GROCER** seriously offended his neighbours by hanging around outside his shop. Normally they wouldn't have minded, but Frederick McLure had been dead for two weeks. He should have been buried earlier, but a thunderstorm flooded his grave in Lubeck, Maine, and his funeral had to wait until it had dried out enough to be redug. In the meantime his coffin rested outside his store. "My father was extremely happy in the store," said his daughter Anne Marie.

**IN FINLAND** obstetrician Dr Arvo Nikula was holding a newborn upside down when it kicked him hard in the right temple, triggering a fatal haemorrhage.

**GRAVEDIGGERS** in Watertown, Massachusetts, were mystified by a stack of bones in the city's Ridgelawn cemetery. They were discovered by staff when they arrived for work at 8am, piled at the cemetery gates. The 13 bones, which appeared to have been buried somewhere else previously, had not been dug up from anywhere in Ridgelawn or neighbouring cemeteries, and came with no indication of their identity.

**PENSIONERS** June and Leonard Collins were horrified to discover their neighbour's plan for his wife's eternal resting place – a plot in his back garden three yards from their bedroom window. When Frances Jackson, 56, died of cancer her husband Peter announced that they wanted a quiet family funeral without undertakers and wished to mourn their loss privately at their home in Pasture Crescent, Knaresborough, Yorkshire. He buried her in his garden under a pagoda he'd previously constructed to shelter his wife from the sun. The Collins's didn't share Mr Jackson's enthusiasm for ecological interment – they went shopping while the funeral took place. "When they bury human beings under your window, it's time something was done about it. It's made us both sick," Leonard said, complaining it had knocked thousands off the value of their semi.

# *Medical Massacre*

**In cases like these, it seems the terms 'Health' and 'Medicine' are only tenuously connected.**

**LIONEL BUCKLEY**, 86, was hurled from an air bed in the burns unit of Manchester's Withington Hospital when an electric pump blew up; he was found dead on the other side of the room. Air beds are used to protect patients from bed sores.

**WHEN** Ronald Eynon, 50, was being treated for breathing difficulties at Prince Philip Hospital in Llanelli, it wasn't just the bed that exploded: it was the patient. He pulled the blankets over his head, slipped off his oxygen mask, lit a cigarette and went up in flames. During the dash to the burns unit at Swansea's Morriston Hospital, he kept asking for a smoke. He died of shock a month later. Also experiencing a surprising ignition was Alberto Alvadoros, 34, who exploded when surgeons in Guayaquil, Ecuador, used a laser scalpel to open him up. Heat from the instrument ignited methane in his gut, causing a ball of flame. Operating staff suffered minor injuries and shock.

**A SPIRIT HEALER'S** unreliable advice about backache led to the death of a Brazilian woman. She set light to her bath of alcohol and ammonia and went up in flames. Elsewhere, four Mexican women taking part in a witchcraft ceremony suffocated as they prepared a concoction of ammonia and smouldering herbs to drive away evil spirits in Mexico City on 14 November 1996. Three were found dead from asphyxiation; the fourth died later in hospital.

**IN AN APPARENT** case of ostension (folklore becoming actual news), wealthy Charles Felder, 71, died after his cleaner, 47-year-old Pauline Jassey, unplugged his life-support machine to use the vacuum cleaner in his bedroom in Dallas, Texas. In a similar incident 14 patients, including four newborn babies in incubators, died after a rat gnawed through the wiring of Catarino Rivas hospital in San Pedro Sula, northern Honduras, and cut off the electricity. Six died when the power was cut to their life-support machines and the short circuit killed the rat.

**GARY HARMON**, 47, died on 10 September 1997, a day after a nine-day stay in St Joseph Mercy-Oakland Hospital in Pontiac, Michigan, where he was being treated for asthma and emphysema. After returning home, he complained about having something he couldn't cough up stuck in his throat. He died in hospital two hours later, having choked on a latex surgical glove. In Brussels, health freak Franz Heinan choked to death on a handful of vitamin pills after lecturing friends on their eating habits.

**ANOTHER** anomalous digestive intrusion saw off Annemarie Jones, 37, a machinist from Birmingham, who was taken to Selly Oak hospital with abdominal pains and died shortly afterwards. Surgeons found her false tooth and its dental plate (the size of a palm) in her inflamed lower colon; they had failed to spot it on the X-rays. When it had disappeared three months earlier, she thought she had lost it, according to her brother, Francis.

**RALPH BREGOS** waited two years for a heart transplant. When news came through to his home in Kentucky that a donor was available, Ralph, 40, got so excited that he had a massive heart attack and died.

**HEART BY-PASS PATIENT** Walter Fryer was crushed to death when a 1.5-ton tree branch fell on him during a fund-raising trek for the hospital which had saved his life. Fryers, 54, died instantly and four others, including his wife, were seriously hurt when the 50ft branch broke away from the 160-year-old beech tree. There was not a breath of wind. Fifty members of the newly-formed Take Heart Club were on a three-mile trek along a leafy lane in Aberford, West Yorkshire, to raise cash for the heart unit at Leeds General Infirmary.

**IN AN ATTEMPT** to cure Maria Mendoza's fear of heights, psychiatrist Ed Cabrillo took her up 20 floors of a Brazilian office block. She had nothing to worry about: all she had to do was just walk into that lift. Maria bit her lip, took a step forward, and plunged to her death. They hadn't noticed the warning signs that the lift was under repair.

**A FILIPINO** who stabbed and beat a surgeon to death for reattaching his penis was publicly beheaded in Saudi Arabia. Joe Solino Jimero, who cut off his own penis because he wanted to become a woman, killed Rashid Abu Jabal after finding the organ reattached.

**PENIS TROUBLE** led to the demise of four New York men. For two years they swallowed an aphrodisiac called 'Rock Hard', thought to have been imported from Hong Kong, instead of rubbing it on their genitals. The American Food and Drug Administration blamed the deaths on poor labelling. The product was said to contain dried toad secretions and a steroid. Oral ingestion caused vomiting and erratic heartbeat.

**TWO WITCHDOCTORS** in Zimbabwe who claimed they could cure AIDS have died from the disease after having sex with patients they believed they had cured.

**CUI TINGXUN**, a teacher in China's Shandong province, was practising the esoteric healing art of qigong with his wife when he suddenly attempted to gouge her eyes out, saying he had received instructions from a 'greater being' to change her facial features. Cui then attacked his wife's jaw with his teeth, saying her mouth smelled badly, before finally decapitating her with a meat cleaver. Police found him holding the shoulders of his wife's torso, exhorting her to sprout a new head.

**A MAN** who stuffed two tampons up his nostrils to try and stop his snoring suffocated in his sleep on 23 January. Labourer Mark Gleeson, 26, of Headley Down, Hampshire, weighed 20 stone and had been told by doctors his snoring was incurable; a car crash eight years earlier had left him with sinus problems. On the night he died, he was staying with his girlfriend Tracey Lambert in Haslemere, Surrey. After drinking wine and taking a few sleeping tablets, he agreed with Tracey to stick two of her tampons up his nose and secured them with tape before going to sleep on her sofa.

**IN HUNAN** province, China, an 85-year-old woman committed suicide because she thought that because she had started menstruating at such an age, she was possessed by devils.

**EGYPTIAN** farm worker Susu Borai Mohammad, 22, accidentally swallowed some ants when she took a swig of water. She went home and swallowed some insecticide to kill the ants, but suffered diarrhoea and convulsions and died immediately after being taken to hospital in the Qena district of Cairo.

**FARMER** Ismail Ayyildiz told drinking companions in the western Turkish province of Edirne that he would shoot out an aching tooth, but the DIY dentistry proved fatal. The bullet left his mouth via the top of his head. He was rushed to hospital, but died a few hours later. Also blowing it spectacularly on the dental front was a labourer in Chon Buri, Thailand, who got drunk, tied an aching tooth with string to a pole and pulled it out without a painkiller. The stress caused his blood pressure to soar and Cha, 40, bled to death.

**SOME DEATHS** defy medical science altogether. Angela Wagstaff, 34, a former nurse at Bristol's Southmead hospital who had drink and mental health problems, was found dead at her home in Hereford after an injection of 1,000–3,000 units of insulin. Such a massive overdose would have needed about 20 syringes to administer, but she had only one puncture mark on her right hip. No syringe was found and there were no signs of a struggle. David Walwyn, who shared his home with Mrs Wagstaff, denied killing her. In July, the Hereford coroner recorded an open verdict: "There seem to be so many inconsistencies," he said.

**A JOBLESS** man who died after becoming addicted to television seems to have lost the will to live. Andrew Thomas, an apparently healthy 27-year-old from Maerdy, South Wales, was made redundant from a supermarket in 1992. When he failed to get another job, he spent every waking moment of the next four years in front of the TV. He got dressed once a week when he went to sign on for his benefits. The day before he died, he got out of bed at noon and watched TV for 14 hours. He was found dead in bed the next morning. Within a week of his death, two job offers arrived in the post. A pathologist told the inquest that the cause of death was 'unascertainable' and a verdict of death by natural causes was recorded.

**PHILLIPA EVERLEIGH,** 49, noticed her car rolling forwards in a car park in Marlborough, Wiltshire. She reached over to apply the handbrake and bruised her arm. After four days the bruise became painful; she was given painkillers and her arm was put in a sling, but her condition deteriorated. She died in hospital three days later. Home Office pathologist Albert Goonetilleke said the cause of death was a fat embolism, where fat cells burst and are released into the bloodstream. "It is very, very rare," he told the inquest in Swindon. "I have only seen it three times in 30 years' practice."

**TONY NEWMAN**, a mentally-handicapped 25-year-old Smethwick man, was found dead of multiple injuries on the Wolverhampton-Birmingham railway line. Newman had told a friend he was suicidal and his injuries were consistent with having been hit by a slow-moving train. This was impossible, as the signalmen were on strike and no trains had run on the night of his death, and the puzzled coroner returned an open verdict.

**A PART-TIME** soldier 'drowned' on dry land during a canoe-ing course in Perthshire in August 1993. The inquest heard how Steve O'Hara, 19, was under water for 15 seconds while righting a capsized canoe. He came ashore and sat down for about 10 minutes before complaining that he felt cold. Seconds later, he collapsed in front of horrified colleagues. Water in his lungs had cut off the supply of oxygen to his brain, and he died of pulmonary and cerebral odema.

**A SIX-YEAR-OLD** boy collapsed in the playground at Coley Park Primary School in Reading on 14 January 1998. Despite attempts to resuscitate the child, he died at the Royal Berkshire Hospital. "There were no visible injuries," said a police source. A year earlier, on 20 January 1997, eight-year-old Joanna Canlin collapsed and died in the same playground. No cause of death was ever established.

**MOTORWAY LABOURER** Michael Cuthbert, 43, came into contact with an unspecified chemical being used at road-works on the A2 at Gravesend in Kent and collapsed on the way to another roadworks site in Faversham. He was taken to the Medway Hospital in Gillingham where an emergency team tried to resuscitate him. As they did so staff and patients broke out in rashes and struggled for breath as fumes spread through the emergency treatment cubicles. The crisis was exacerbated by a power failure at the accident centre, which closed down the ventilation system, forcing a full scale evacuation as resus-citation attempts continued. Cuthbert, a Scot working for a gang contracted by EFM Ltd, a West Sussex roadworks firm, died several days later of a heart attack, but it is unclear whether this was a direct result of the chemical contamination.

**THE *SCOTS LAW TIMES*** printed a wince-making letter from the Prostate Help Association in 1995. This read "Professional men have many types of stress which affect their lives, many are discussed and written about in the media. One aspect however is not discussed and this led to the unfortunate death of a professional man last year. A 63-year-old accountant attempted DIY surgery on his enlarged prostate with a length of electric wire and subsequently died following an infection." Ouch!

# *This Sporting Life*

**Huntin', fishin', shootin' and ... er ... golf are all lethal in their own way.**

**ANGELO MAULE**, 58, was killed by the still-struggling trout he had just caught striking him across the head. He was knocked onto the rocks at Val di Susa and died.

**A RUSSIAN** hunter and a bear are thought to have killed each other in a struggle. Searchers discovered Yuri Smakotin's body next to the carcass of a shot brown bear about 60 miles from the village of Kukan in the Far Eastern Khabarovsk region of Siberia. Danilo Maggioni, 38, shot a wild boar near his home in Varese, Northern Italy. Searchers later found both the hunted and hunter dead; the enraged boar had hurled Maggioni into a ravine before dying.

**A SERB** man was bitten to death by a badger he was hunting when the animal turned on him, ripped a piece of flesh from his thigh and severed a vein. Dragan Ckonjevic died within minutes from loss of blood.

**EINNER DAHL**, 54, of Minton, Saskatchewan, killed a buck deer while hunting on 5 November 1994. Later, as he tried to move the deer at a relative's home in Celon, south of Regina, the antler punctured his leg and hit an artery. He died before he could get help.

**CHRIS BOWIE**, 29, from West Palm Beach, Florida, was dragged to his death by the fish he was trying to catch. He was pulled 30 feet under by a giant blue marlin when his hands became tangled in the line during a contest off North Carolina.

**A POACHER** electrocuting fish in a Polish lake died when he fell into the water and suffered the same fate as his quarry. The 24-year-old man was one of four who had attached a cable to a fishing net and a high-voltage electricity line. Outside Moscow, another poacher suffered a similar fate, dying after he tried to catch fish by putting a live cable into a pond. He forgot to disconnect the electricity before collecting the fish.

**THREE** Fijian fishermen choked to death on live fish in 1994–95. All three tried to kill their catch by biting its head. A fisherman from the island of Rabi was the first fatality in December 1994. On 14 January, a fish head got lodged in the throat of Samueal Taoba, 50, from a village near Savusavu on the island of Vanua Levu. Its spines lodged in his gullet and he suffocated before his friends could pull it out. Serupepeli Lumelume, 22, died in exactly the same way on 14 February, while fishing in a river near Narvosa on the island of Viti Levu.

**FIJI** is rich in fish fatalities: perhaps they're starting to fight back there? Kinijioji Vindovi, 69, and four other Fijian fishermen were asleep on their 24ft boat anchored in open seas when a nine-foot shark leapt aboard and attacked Vindovi, nearly tearing off his right leg and right hand. He died shortly after reaching a village hospital. Another Fijian fisherman bled to death on 15 March when a surface-skimming swordfish leapt at his night lamp and stabbed him in the face. Meli Kalakulu, 18, of Gau Island, had been night fishing near Suva in the South Pacific.

**GOLFER** David Bailey, 40, of Clondalkin, Co Dublin, was killed by a rat which ran up his trouser leg as he hunted for a lost ball at Caddockstown golf course in Co Kildare. He startled the animal when he jumped into a ditch at the first hole. It shot up his leg and urinated on him. His golf partners advised him to take a shower immediately, but he laughed off the encounter, saying he had no cuts or bites. He took a shower four hours later after finishing the round. However, before this he had touched his leg and smoked a cigar. Doctors believe that the deadly Weil's disease carried by the rat was passed from his fingers to his mouth. He was admitted to a Dublin hospital with severe jaundice two weeks later, but died in intensive care when his kidneys collapsed.

**JEREMY T. BRENNO**, 16, slammed his Number Three golf club against a bench after making a bad shot at the Kingsboro Golf Club in Gloversville, New York. He bled to death after the club's broken shaft snapped back and pierced his pulmonary vein. A 10-year-old boy from Hove, Sussex, died when a friend hit him on the head with a golf club while playing on a sea-front course in the town. Days later, 16-year-old Robert Hearfield was killed during golf practice in Middlesborough, Cleveland, when a ball struck by a friend hit him on the temple, causing a fatal blood clot.

**ELDERLY** golfer Jean Potevan threw his golf bag into a lake after missing three putts on the final hole of a disastrous round at Orléans (or Lyons) in France. Realising that his car keys were in the bag, he waded in fully clothed but drowned when he got entangled in weeds as he dived under the water. According to fellow player Henri Levereau, his last words were: "I'm going back for the keys, but I'm leaving the clubs down there."

**IN TOKYO**, golfer Takeo Niyama, 43, lost his grip when his partner giggled after he sliced a stroke. He charged the man and beat him over the head with his club until he was dead. He was arrested for murder.

**A TRAINEE** bungee jumper panicked as he fell, reached out and knocked his instructor to his death in an amusement park in Nagoya, Japan. Police were considering criminal charges.

**GLIDER PILOT** Seth Daniels of Carefree, Arizona, came to an unexpected end when he made a desert landing near Phoenix. As he came down his wing clipped a giant cactus, causing it to crash onto the glider's cockpit, killing him instantly. For 18 years, Charles Cooke devoted every minute of his spare time to building his own light aircraft. When he finally finished it and the great day arrived for its first flight, Cooke gathered his friends in Watsonville, California, to watch him take off. Moments later they also saw the end of both the flight and Charles as his DIY plane hurtled to the ground in a ball of flame.

**TWO** boy scouts were killed during an attempt to get into the Guinness Book of Records by staging a giant tug-of-war involving 650 people. The thick nylon rope snapped and whipped back violently at the contest in Frankfurt, causing the teams to collapse. A nine-year-old boy died at the scene and a 10-year-old several days later. At least 24 others were injured.

**A 33-YEAR-OLD** man used in dwarf-tossing contests died of brain damage after landing on his head too many times. The diminutive Australian earned his living as a missile in pub competitions. He retired, but became "sullen and aggressive," according to friends.

**SECONDS** after bowling his final over in his retirement match, cricket veteran Jack Swain, 73, collapsed and died at his club in Cuckfield, Sussex. Despite efforts by his team-mates and wife Peggy, he could not be revived.

**EMIL KIJEK**, 79, hit the first hole-in-one of his life at the golf club in Rehoboth, Massachusetts, where he had played for 30 years, then jubilantly walked on to the next hole. The excitement, however, proved too much. At the next tee, he approached the ball, rolled his eyes, said "Oh no," then collapsed dead of a heart attack. In Hemet, California, another golfing oldster, Peter Sedore, 83, was rather luckier; he still dropped dead on the course, but he was four years older and had just scored his 18th hole-in-one. He shouted: "Hooray, number 18!", then collapsed into the arms of his golf partner Bill Rutledge, dead from an aneurism.

**WHEN** 77-year-old Jimmy Hogg took his turn to drop dead on a golf course, in his case without a hole-in-one to see him off, his four golfing pals watched the ambulance taking him away drive off then returned to their game, finishing the round. One member of the club in Kinghorn, Fife, stormed: "What they did was out of order. They could have cancelled their round for the day." But Jack Ketchin, 77, insisted: "I'm sure Jimmy would have wanted us to continue."

**SOME PEOPLE** don't just hang around waiting for other golfers to drop dead; they give them a helping hand. Richard Stephens, 51, was playing with his 12-year-old son on the New Berlin Hills golf course in Wisconsin when their slow play enraged the group following them. Eventually, as Mr Stephens searched for a ball his son had hit into a creek, they confronted him and a fight broke out, during which the disgruntled golfers kicked Stephens to death.

**A FOOTBALL FAN** from Seville, Spain, was not about to let anything as trivial as death keep him from the game. As a final wish, the un-named fan asked his son to take his ashes to every game played by his club, Real Betis. The son went one better. He renewed his father's season ticket, so the ashes have their own seat.

**DURING** the 1994 World Cup, a 53-year-old woman stabbed her partner to death with a pair of scissors when he forced her to stay up to watch his country Sweden's game against Cameroon. After the killing, the woman fell asleep. Amazingly (or perhaps not so amazingly, given people's obsession with football), two other fans watching the game with the couple did not notice what had happened and continued cheering their team on, falling asleep after the match too.

**OLYMPIC WRESTLING** was rocked by the death of three up-and-coming young stars in training. Jeff Reese, 21, was trying to get his weight down 8lbs to 150lbs by training in a boiling hot gym while in a rubber wet suit, when he dropped dead from the exertion; Joe LaRosa, 22, and Billy Jack Saylor from North Carolina followed hard on his heels doing the same thing. The head of the investigating commission said: "We always used to practise wearing our rubber suits. It never did us any harm."

**THE RACING YACHT** *Happy Ending* was discovered floating 700 miles off Land's End by the U.S. container ship *Sealand Quality*, with the body of its owner Gerald Hardesty, 63, on board. There was no sign of his wife, Carol, 60, who had also been on board. The rescue ship was prevented from taking the yacht in tow or recovering the body because of extreme weather. A spokesman from the Falmouth coastguards, who co-ordinated the recovery, said: "It's weird – the yacht was located at exactly 13.13 hours on the 13th day of the month." They found no sign of the woman's body and suspected she had been lost overboard in a storm, but could find no injuries which would explain the man's death.

**FELIPE ORTIZ**, 48, fishing in Colombia cast a line into the teeth of a gale – and suffocated when the baited hook blew back and lodged in his throat. Efforts to save him by slapping his back failed.

**THE MYTH** that left-handed people die younger than right-handers was exploded by research involving left-handed cricketers carried out at the University of Durham. Professor John Aggleton examined the lives of 5,960 first-class cricketers born between 1840 and 1960 and compared the longevity of the 1,132 who bowled left-handed to that of their right-handed colleagues. Cricketers were chosen because comprehensive cricketing encyclopaedias clearly specified each player's bowling hand. When the results were analysed the researchers found no significant difference in survival linked with handedness – except in times of war. In wartime 5.4 per cent of left-handed cricketers died in action compared to 3 per cent of right-handed cricketers, possibly because military training and equipment is designed for right-handers. When deaths due to warfare were removed from the equation the mortality curves for both handers were almost identical.

CHAPTER ELEVEN

# *Fiendish Fur and Feathers*

**It doesn't pay to underestimate our four-legged friends (or our two-legged ones for that matter).**

**IN AN ATTEMPT** to rescue a chicken on 31 July 1995, a young Egyptian farmer descended a 60-foot well in the village of Nazlat Imara, 240 miles south of Cairo. He drowned, apparently, after an undercurrent in the water pulled him down. His sister and two brothers went in one by one to help him, but also drowned. Two elderly farmers then came to help, but suffered the same fate. The bodies of all six were later pulled out, along with the chicken, which was the only survivor. In a similar incident, a chicken fell down a 25-foot well in Lam Dong province, Vietnam, so Nguyen Minh Chien, 11, tried to rescue it. When he didn't emerge, his brother Nguyen Thanh Vuong and a neighbour, Nong Van Dai, went to investigate. This time they suffocated in gases which had built up in the well.

**THREE MEN** trying to lift a 44ft-long irrigation pipe in Linden, California, to free a rabbit which had scurried inside were electrocuted when the pipe touched a 12,000-volt electrical wire.

**THE MUTILATED** corpse of Frans Jaumotte was found in the henhouse of his farm near Brussels. Police found no chicken feed at the farm. Jaumotte's 200 chickens had presumably attacked him and pecked out his eyes and heart.

**MELANY PAULA CAMPOS**, 60, was discovered dead by her sister Lelys, beneath four bags of dog food which had fallen on her. The sisters shared a home with about 40 abandoned dogs which they looked after in the Sylmar area of Los Angeles. Lelys said she knew something was awry when she got home and neighbours told her the dogs had been barking for a number of hours. Elsewhere, Carol Williams, 54, of Townhill, Swansea, suffocated when she fell face-down into her dog's bowl and its rim pressed against her neck. The inquest heard she was three times over the drink-drive limit.

**FRANK AUSTIN**, 43, bled to death in his Manchester house on 29 November 1996 when paramedics were prevented from getting inside the door by 12 of his 17 rottweilers. He had been stabbed in a domestic altercation. He rang for an ambulance, but the crew feared they would be killed by the dogs if they ventured inside. "One of the rottweilers was particularly aggressive and kept jumping against the windows," said a spokesman. After two hours, the police destroyed the male dog, but by then Mr Austin was dead. In Bonn, Otto the rottweiler defended his owner against paramedics for 12 minutes after he collapsed with a coronary. By the time they got Otto to move, the 68-year-old was dead. Still, it's the thought that counts.

**TAKING** a more direct route was the 'trained' two-year-old lion which pawnbroker Luis Barraco bought to guard his shop in Rio de Janeiro, Brazil, against burglars. When he opened up the next morning, it killed him. Never underestimate lions. Near Johannesburg, South Africa, a late-night drinker popped out for a stroll in a game reserve to clear his head … and was promptly eaten by five of them.

**RED THUNDER CLOUD**, a Native American from Northbridge, Massachusetts, caused considerable problems when he died. He was the last speaker of the Catawba language, and left behind a dog, Blazing Arrow, trained to respond only to commands in Catawba, so no one could control him. In a desperate effort to deal with the animal, a search was mounted to locate some usable fragments of Catawba. When this report was written, only one command had been found: "Tanty!" (meaning "Seize!") was not proving to be of much help.

**JANET SMITH**, 28, walked into a grocery store in Gresham, Oregon, on 21 August 1994, holding a knife to the throat of her Siamese cat, and sat down in an aisle. Told by police to drop the knife, she threatened to kill the cat. Suddenly, she jumped up and began walking towards the police, who sprayed her with pepper mace. She then raised the knife above her head and charged at the police, who shot her dead. The cat escaped into the store and could not be found.

**FARMER** Yiannis Karayannopoulos, 87, from Oropedio, near Grevena in northern Greece, believed his cat had been stolen by his neighbour, Thomas Koletsos, so he shot him dead as he left for work. Mr Koletsos's wife, Chrysanthi, heard the shot, rushed out and was shot dead in turn. Karayannopoulos then turned the gun on himself. The cat returned later in the day.

**MAXINE ANNE KEGERREIS**, 79, died in Allegan, Michigan, while trying to exercise her dog and mow the lawn at the same time. She drowned in a pond after becoming entangled in the dog chain attached to her riding mower. She apparently tried to back up when the chain and mower snagged, and fell into the water with the dog, which also drowned.

**A 66-YEAR-OLD** Croatian woman was killed by her grandson's 80lb Staffordshire terrier whose life she had spared two years earlier. Katarina Paunovic of Novska, southeast of Zagreb, was sitting on her porch on 8 June 1997 when the four-year-old pet went for her neck, severing an artery. Her grandson had wanted to put the animal down when it bit him, but she had successfully pleaded for its life.

**BIRD LOVER** Tom Stones, 25, marched with supporters into an animal refuge in Nairobi, Kenya, in a bid to save it from closure. Unwittingly, he walked between a male ostrich and its mate. The nine-feet-tall male rushed up to Stones and delivered a fatal blow to his head. Ostriches are exceedingly strong, but also exceedingly dim. Ouma (or Anna) Hendriks, 63, was attacked by an enraged ostrich on a farm in Joostenbergvlakte, about 25 miles from Cape Town. Her husband Abraham, 65, watched helplessly as she was kicked and stomped on for about an hour. He managed to flag down help after the ostrich left, and the couple were taken to hospital, where Mrs Hendriks died four days later. The attack occurred when the couple, who lived on an adjacent farm, walked through an ostrich herd on the Lekkerwater farm on their way to visit friends.

**VICHAI THONGTO**, 30, of Ratchaburi province in Thailand, was killed by a peacock, his pet for eight years. He was feeding four caged birds when the sole male clawed his head, causing a blood clot. He died in hospital on 7 April 1997. His family would have curried the peacock out of revenge, but were too fond of it. All four birds were given to a local zoo.

**BAT CATCHER** Gumilid Lantod was alone in the jungle in April 1998 on Mindoro Island in the Philippines when a 23ft python bit him on the foot and squeezed him to death. Pythons can tell when their victims are dead when they can no longer feel a pulse. Then the monster swallowed the 154lb man. Friends later found the snake and slit it open, finding the father of six already half digested. About three days later, a two-month-old boy was consumed by a python in the Philippines' Cavite province. In Thailand, Manee Saisin, 35, a snake catcher and charmer, was strangled to death by an 11ft boa constrictor he was carrying home round his neck in Phetchaburi, 90 miles south of Bangkok.

**WHEN** a Saudi woman arrived in the eastern city of Dammam to visit her daughter and her new-born child, she complained of 'strange movements' down her back during the journey from the south. Her daughter pulled back her dress to investigate and received a fatal bite from a viper.

**A BRAZILIAN** woman of 52 died after brushing her arm against a caterpillar. Death by caterpillar is now three to six times more common than by snakebite in southern parts of the country, with at least 10 fatalities in the past three years. The killer caterpillars, *Lonomia obliqua*, have hairs containing poison which stop blood clotting. The woman felt burning of the skin, headache and weakness. Over the subsequent two days she developed bruising and vomited. She was hospitalised in a coma and tests showed she suffered bleeding in the brain. She died two days later. The caterpillar population has been growing in rural areas because rats, birds, wasps and their other natural predators have been killed by rapid deforestation and the use of toxic fertilisers.

**A SHEEP** to be sacrificed for the Muslim feast of Al-Adha rushed his executioner, who lost his balance and fell to his death from the top of a four-storey building in Cairo.

**IN QUINTON**, Birmingham, builder Seagan Dawe, 61, was working at the top of a ladder when his workmate Patrick Dowling heard him scream: "Get off! Get off!" and saw him topple from the ladder and crash to his death. He had been savaged by a squirrel which had popped out of the guttering and bitten him in the face.

**A FLY** flew in through the window of a truck being driven by Arthur Tiffit in Broadus, Montana, and into his mouth, causing him to choke and lose control of the vehicle, which crashed killing his 51-year-old wife.

**RACHEL DRAKE**, a headteacher from Southampton, died instantly when a 500lb deer was catapulted onto the roof of her car. Miss Drake, 50, suffered massive head injuries after the stag ran onto the road, was struck by an oncoming vehicle and landed on the roof of Miss Drake's car.

**IN SOUTH AFRICA,** a three-year-old boy and two women were killed in a huge explosion at a game farm caused by an iguana, which had crawled under a fridge and dislodged a pipe.

**AN EXTERMINATOR** called out by widow Opal Bevil to deal with an ant invasion in her garden was himself exterminated ... by the ants he'd come to wipe out. As he approached the eight large ant hills, a massive horde of fire ants swarmed out and covered him from head to foot, killing him with thousands of bites.

**MAURICE SELWYN** also died from an ant bite, but it took only one to kill him. He was tending his cows at Levin in New Zealand when he was bitten by a huge bull ant. While the bite of a bull ant is painful, it is hardly lethal. Selwyn died of fright when he saw the size of the insect which had attacked him. Fright also saw off German model Greeta Shook, 19, who dropped dead in panic after a mouse jumped down her cleavage before a catwalk show in Messina, Sicily, and short-sighted Ellen Morgan had a heart attack and died after mistaking her husband's wig for a rat. He had left it on the table and she thought it was a rodent about to eat a nearby bowl of nuts.

**IN PRAGUE,** Czechoslovakia, a man was jailed for 11 years for strangling a neighbour who ate his dog. The murderer believed his dog had run off, but a friend told him that his neighbour had stolen, skinned and roasted the animal, serving him up for a family meal.

**A RUSSIAN HOUSEWIFE,** aged 39, lost control when her 40-year-old husband returned home from drinking with pals and became abusive. Police said the woman stabbed him in the chest, castrated him and cut him into pieces. She then fed the body to her pigs, but kept the head as a memento for a while before burying it.

**IN GERMANY** a farmer went a step further, getting one of his animals to carry out the murder for him. Josef Meschede, 44, trained his bull Maxi to attack on command, then lured his 40-year-old wife Karolina into the animal's enclosure, knocked her down with a pitchfork and set him on her. Maxi trampled the woman to death, then was immediately put down. Police only became suspicious after Josef tried to cash in £500,000 worth of life insurance policies, which would have paid off the massive debts he had, when they found he had already contacted dating agencies before Karolina's death and that the policies had been taken out without his wife's knowledge, with her signature faked on the forms.

# *Crime and Punishment*

**Vengeance is mine, sayeth the Lord ...**

**ROBERT PUELO**, 32, entered a 7-Eleven convenience store in St Louis on 10 October 1994 and started shouting and cursing. When an employee threatened to call the police, Puelo grabbed a hotdog, stuffed it down his throat and left the store without paying. The police discovered him unconscious and turning purple outside the store. He choked to death on a six-inch piece of sausage jammed in his throat.

**A ROBBERY SUSPECT** who tried to swallow incriminating evidence choked to death on a $50 bill. The man collapsed in the back seat of a patrol car in Buffalo, New York, on 25 April 1995 about an hour after he was caught attacking a woman in a supermarket parking lot. Nine days earlier in Australia, Adam Kane Morris, a 23-year-old paranoid schizophrenic from Kew, near Sydney, had choked to death on a wad of 10 $50 notes which he had swallowed during a fit in the bath.

**A MAN** who was doing a year for robbery at St Helier Correctional Centre in Muswellbrook was met by his girl-friend at 8am on the day of his first day-release. They went to a caravan park where, about 9am, he collapsed and died during sexual intercourse.

**A FLASHER** exposing himself to women on the New York subway was killed by a train when he forgot to pull up his trousers before running away. He tripped and fell on the track as the train pulled into the station. In Milan, another flasher was killed by a bus when he stepped into the road to expose himself to the bus queue.

**RAPIST** Jean-Pierre Lavreau pounced on a victim in a club car park in Marseilles, France, ripping her mini-skirt off, but dropped dead of a heart-attack when he saw what was under-neath. The blonde was a well-endowed transvestite and the shock was just too much for the over-excited Lavreau, who was thought to have committed at least 13 previous attacks in the city.

**AN IRAQI** terrorist, Khay Rahnajet, was supposedly hoist by his own petard when the bomb he had posted with insufficient stamps was returned. It blew up when he picked it up. A nice story, if a little short on detail.

**AN UN-NAMED** Moscow company director fell ill, was admitted to hospital and died from what looked curiously like radiation poisoning. When other employees of the Karton-Tara packaging company fell ill, the deputy bought a dosimeter and discovered levels of radioactivity in the director's and sur-rounding offices up to 1.5 million times higher than expected, and a lump of radioactive material in the back of his chair.

Police blamed the Muscovite Mafia.

**LAM TING-MING**, 56, died after four hours' questioning by police about two murders. The post-mortem revealed broken ribs, a torn liver and severe internal and external bruising, but Lam had died of a heart attack. Investigating officers suggested that his death might have been self-inflicted, as Lam was a follower of sundar. Believers invite supernatural forces into their bodies and then, to prove the forces' strength, stab and beat themselves up. The wounds do not appear until the believer's death.

**GARETH DAVIES**, 31, choked to death when a heavy patio door landed on his neck as he attempted to break into the house of solicitor Norman Hughes in Pontyclun, Mid-Glamorgan. He levered open the 12ft by 6ft 'tilt and slide' glass door and tried to prop it open with an iron bar. As he crawled feet-first under the door, it swung back and trapped him by the neck. Mr Hughes found the body early the next morning. At first he thought it was a Guy Fawkes dummy. In Los Angeles, a burglar died after he broke into a house which was being fumigated and was overcome by the chemicals.

**AN ARSONIST** boiled to death in Manila when he hid in a drum of water to protect himself from a fire he started. Renato Salazar, an employee of a haulage firm, had entered his company's kitchen, opened two gas tanks and then hidden inside the water-filled drum before tossing a lighted match at the tanks. The fire destroyed the two-storey building.

**ANTHONY IRVIN** must have thought that robbing a blind man would be easy; but Courtney Beswick, aged 28 and blind since birth, flipped him over his shoulder and put him in a wrestling hold until police arrived. Irvin was taken to hospital in Philadelphia, but was pronounced dead of neck injuries. In 1987, Mr Beswick was named Most Valuable Wrestler for the Eastern Atlantic Association of Schools for the Blind.

**LAURENCE BAKER**, 47, a murderer in jail since 1983 who had been spared the electric chair 10 years earlier, was electrocuted in a Pittsburgh jail when he sat on a stainless steel commode watching TV and wearing a set of badly-wired, home-made headphones. The accident happened between 10pm on 1 January 1997 and 1.30am the following morning. It was an eerie precursor to the death of murderer Michael Anderson Godwin, 28, on 6 March 1988. Anderson had escaped the electric chair in Columbia, South Carolina. He was sitting naked on the metal commode in his cell mending the headphones on his TV when he electrocuted himself by biting through a wire. The headphones are required to prevent the sound from disturbing other prisoners.

**ROBERT BRECHEEN** took an overdose of sedatives and was rushed to hospital from his Oklahoma prison cell to have his stomach pumped. After he recovered he was returned to the prison, where he was executed by lethal injection. The director of the State Corrections Department said: "Certainly, there's irony," while the husband of Brecheen's victim said grimly: "It wasn't his job to take his life."

**TORGE CZAR**'s plan to burgle a Warsaw jewellers involved tunnelling through a wall and into a safe on the other side. A miscalculation took him into a food factory, when he fell into a vat of spinach and drowned.

**TWO RUSSIAN** policemen shot each other dead on 7 March

1997 in a case of mistaken identity while trying to arrest suspected robbers. One group of policemen in the town of Nizhny Novgorod, east of Moscow, mistook another group for the crooks in the dark after they refused an order to drop their weapons. In Rock Island, Illinois, auxiliary police officer Captain Richard Shurtz died of injuries suffered in a car wreck while trying to drive himself to hospital. He had been demonstrating how another officer had been fatally shot three days before when he shot himself.

**FORMER POLICEMAN** Arthur Smith, 56, was hired by a friend to murder his ex-wife Rita Quam, who lived in the Colorado town of Edwards, 7,500ft up in the Rockies. Wearing a false beard and moustache, asthma sufferer Smith tried to shoot 53-year-old Quam, but the thin mountain air made him wheeze so heavily that he missed, so he tried to bludgeon her to death with a rock. Before he could hit her, however, the strain became too much and he fell backwards clutching his heart, dead of a massive asthma-induced coronary.

**ROMANIAN PENSIONERS** Teodor Tacu, 65, and Elena Sambursachi were robbed and murdered at their flat in Cluj by four 20-year-old boys and a girl. The murderers, who were arrested the next day, had cut out their victims' eyes and cut their throats. When asked why they had done this, they said: "We cut the eyes and throats in order that the police could not discover our images on the optic nerve of the victims and our names on their vocal cords. We have learned that from crime pictures." And a lot of good it did them.

**IN ROME,** three youths faced life imprisonment for scaring an elderly man to death. The terrified pensioner died of a heart attack after they sneaked into his home and put a corpse in his bed.

**IN GENEVA**, a mugger making his getaway after attacking an elderly man was brought up short when the man's schoolboy neighbour Gustav Krause killed him with an accurately-aimed, hard-packed snowball. Elsewhere in Switzerland, Amy and Christopher Baerlocher were murdered at their village home three weeks after they had left New York because they thought it was too violent.

**SUSPECTED KILLER** Elmer Sinarillos, accused of hacking two women and two children to death, climbed a tree to avoid capture by a pack of angry villagers in the southern Philippines, but was killed when his pursuers chopped it down with a chainsaw. Sinarillos crashed to the ground and broke his back. Also taking an unexpected fall was peeping tom Salvatore Malerba, 40, who was hiding on top of a cliff to watch topless girls through binoculars. In his excitement he didn't notice the edge and plunged 100ft to his death. At least he died with a smile on his face.

**MIGUEL GONZALEZ**, 32, died when his family agreed to switch off his life-support machine after it became clear he had no hope of emerging from his coma. He had been beaten senseless by Charles Mahuka, his anger-management counsellor, at a class he had been ordered to attend for assaulting his girlfriend. Witnesses said Gonzales arrived at the class drunk and disrupted it. Mahuka lost his temper and hit Gonzales, knocking him to the ground, then continued beating him until he was senseless.

# *Do It Yourself*

**According to statistics, suicide is becoming an evermore popular way out.**

**THE VILLAGE** of Over Stratton, near Yeovil, was temporarily declared a no-go area after retired Falklands hero Lieutenant-Commander Ian Cobbold, 60, killed himself. He adapted his vacuum cleaner to pump rather than suck, left a couple of notes explaining the chemical hazards, took an overdose of sleeping pills and filled the house with a nerve gas derived from rat poison. Twelve people were rushed to hospital, and his neighbours and the local playschool were evacuated.

**CHRISTEL R**, 63, from Beverungen, Germany, tired of her drunken husband and decided to shuffle off the mortal coil via a circular saw. Hubby Karl tired of waiting for his breakfast and went to look for her. He found both halves in the toolshed. Similar results were achieved by a 36 year-old-man in Belmez, Spain, whose offed himself by handcuffing his arms to opposite sides of a drawbridge and waiting for it to go up. He was torn in two.

**CORY QUINN**, from Sydney, Australia, committed suicide by locking himself in his estranged wife Mary's freezer when she went on holiday. His note for the 20-stone woman said: "Gorge on this, you fat pig!" At the other end of the scale, Steven Jean Hoover taped aluminium foil over the windows of his flat to make it quiet and dark, wrote a note listing the times he had tried to commit suicide, arranged painkillers and vitamins on his bedside table and stopped eating. When his apartment was sold 18 months later, the new owners found Hoover's mummified body lying in bed.

**MANIC DEPRESSIVE** Emily Sheaves, 37, committed suicide by drinking three gallons of tap water. The Devon woman fell into a coma and died the same day.

**DINO VANNINI**, 74, of Empoli, Italy, doused his car and 220m lire with petrol, set them alight and went out in a blaze of glory. Even more glorious was the departure of Bohumil Sole, 63, one of the creators of the plastic explosive Semtex, who died on 25 May 1997 in a blast that destroyed the main bathhouse at the Czech spa of Jesenik. There were 20 injuries and six people were hospitalised with burns. The police said Sole's death was suicide but didn't elaborate.

**EQUALLY SPECTACULAR**, if less successful, was the suicide of James Kimble, 32, who tried to kill himself by turning on the gas and lighting a match. He ended up with a broken leg and burns; however, five houses were flattened and 35 business properties damaged. Also highly pyrotechnic, if unintentionally, was the suicide attempt of Lucia Cargnio, of Palermo, who lit a ciggie while trying to gas herself. She survived the explosion but three other people died and another 10 were injured. A similar result was achieved by Djamila Kinzi, 22, who had been unlucky in love. She intended gassing herself at her home in Albi, France, but changed her mind. She opened the windows, lit a cigarette and the resulting blast killed two people and injured a further six. She was jailed for manslaughter. A Bordeaux man who also changed his mind and had a smoke instead was treated for burns. Do these people never read the papers?

**NORMA GALETTO**, 42, of Pavia, Italy, also cocked up her fiery finale. She decided to end her life by drenching herself in petrol and setting herself alight, but changed her mind and dived into the River Ticino, where she drowned. She couldn't swim.

**SORT OF** failing dismally was jilted lover Edward Hand, who tried to make a dramatic exit by blowing himself away in front of his love rival. He put the gun to his chin and pulled the trigger, but the bullet ricocheted off his teeth into the head of his rival, killing him instantly. Florida police arrested Hand and charged him with manslaughter, kidnapping and assault.

**A GUATEMALAN** gun salesman committed suicide by hurling himself into a pit of jaguars in Guatemala City's zoo after accidentally shooting a customer dead. Paco Cazanga, 32, was rescued from the pit by firefighters, who used extinguishers to repel four jaguars, but he died later in hospital. Also choosing an animal exit was jilted lover Scott McCraw, 37, from Long Island. He committed suicide on 21 February 1994 by agitating Shakey, his pet rattlesnake, until it bit him. He died in a field from heart failure and the snake died of hypothermia. The bodies were not discovered for 19 days.

**A HONG KONG** woman determined to haunt her former boyfriend jumped off a 35-storey block of flats on the fifth anniversary of losing her virginity to him. She wore red, the traditional colour for would-be ghosts.

**SOLICITOR** Linda Harvey, 44, leapt to her death from a third-storey bedroom window in Hastings. An aircraft flight from Paris had left her with a incurable tinnitus when cabin pressure had suddenly dropped and damaged her inner ear. She was en route from Bordeaux, where she had just undergone a successful operation to cure deafness in one ear.

**GENERAL** (a name not a rank) Fleming, 39, committed suicide very thoroughly in Akron, Ohio, on 12 May 1996. He jumped out of his apartment on the 14th floor, shooting himself in the head as he fell. The .38-calibre bullet went out the back of his head as he was upside down and hit an apartment across the courtyard. He landed on the first-storey concrete courtyard in the centre of the building. He left a suicide note, but did not say why he wanted to die.

**ELROD HILL** also managed to shoot himself successfully, and then some. He leant the butt of his semi-automatic AK-47 against the arm of his sofa and pulled the trigger. The bullet entered his head, killing him instantly. It also killed his friend Brian Olesky, who was sitting next to him. Richard Gorby, 35, took someone with him too. He killed himself with carbon monoxide from his car exhaust in Pittsburgh, but the fumes from his garage also wiped out his 86-year-old upstairs neighbour Rowene Ebling as she sat in her bedroom.

**BROADMOOR NURSE** Dominic Noviski, 26, prevented a colleague from committing suicide by confiscating the pills he intended to use ... then killed himself with them.

**FOUL PLAY** was ruled out in the death of Jean Pierre Gagnon, 30, whose frozen body, partly covered in snow, was found on 12 January 1997 by a hiker in a wooded area near the Beechwood Cemetery in Ottawa, Ontario. He had committed suicide by impaling his chest on a broken tree branch and bleeding to death.

**LIFT ENGINEER** James Raynor, 61, of Netherhall, Leicester, tied a noose to the top of an elevator shaft, stood on the lift roof and waited patiently in the dark for it to go down. He was killed when the lift was called to a lower floor. He was depressed after losing his licence for drunk-driving.

**ALSO** organising an off-beat, if appropriate, way to top himself was Geoff Birch, 52, Captain of Bells at St Luke's Church in Sheen near Buxton in the Peak district. Birch was found hanging from his own bell rope by a local farmer. He had apparently silenced the bells so no-one in the village would be alerted to his suicide.

**LALJI ARJANBAI PATEL**, a devout 28-year-old Indian, committed suicide by decapitating himself. He strung a sickle from the roof of a deserted temple; he then lay down to pray, let go of the rope and his head was instantly severed.

**IN EASTLING**, Sussex, a scientist who hanged himself announced the fact to the world with a message on his answering machine saying: "I can't come to the phone at the moment because I'm dead."

**NOVELIST** Alexander Cordell wrote a suicide note then climbed up to the beautiful Horseshoe Pass, near Llangollen, Wales. He was found with photos of his two much-loved wives, both of whom had died, a bottle of brandy and some barbiturates. When a post-mortem was done, however, it was discovered that he had died of a heart attack, probably brought on by the climb. In Northampton 24-year-old Stephen Butler, depressed after a divorce and worrying about debt, drank heavily for a day, then decided to commit suicide. The excitement of making the decision produced such a rush of adrenaline that he dropped dead before he had a chance to act on it.

**TERRY BRAND**, 45, of Bournemouth, took flying lessons for three months before going out for his first solo flight. He took up a £70,000 Piper Warrior PA28, radio'd an apology to the air traffic controllers and plunged his light aircraft into the sea. He left a note saying that he was not depressed but merely following his destiny. Within 10 years his good looks and love of life would have gone.

**CROATIAN** twins committed suicide on the same day without the other knowing. Branko Uhiltil, 57, hanged himself in his house in Lipovljani, 50 miles east of Zagreb; two hours later, his brother Ivan shot himself in his flat.

**THREE JAPANESE** men in their fifties, all from the same company, hanged themselves in separate rooms in the same Tokyo hotel on 26 February 1988. Each was wearing an identical white shirt when found hanging from identical white ropes.

**ALSO IN JAPAN**, a 45-year-old man arrested for allegedly setting fire to his own shop in Hokkaido choked himself to death on toilet paper. Police found him in his cell with 5.5 yards of paper down his throat.

# CHAPTER FOURTEEN

# *Eat, Drink and Die Merry*

**It is said that the road of excess leads to the palace of wisdom … but sometimes it just kills you.**

**MARLENE CORRIGAN**, from El Cerrito, California, allowed her daughter Christina to eat herself to death on 19 November 1996. The 13-year-old weighed 680lb and had lived nude on the living room floor in front of the TV, covered in a sheet. Her thighs were 54in in circumference. She was surrounded by fried chicken boxes and hamburger wrappers and covered in bedsores, bugs and fæces. Her brother said he had not seen her stand up for a couple of months. The cause of death was heart failure due to morbid obesity. Mrs Corrigan had done nothing to curb Christina's weight since abandoning visits to a nutritionist when the girl was seven.

**IN JERUSALEM**, the post-mortem examination of Claudio Mateo Medina, 34, a Franciscan priest from Mexico, found dead in his room at the Church of the Holy Sepulchre, discovered that the man had died of over-eating. Elsewhere, Turkish villager Demker Cevik won a £6 bet by eating a whole barbecued lamb. Ten minutes later he keeled over, dead.

**MILLIONS** of Japanese people start their new year with a zoni soup containing mochi rice cakes. The mochi are rubbery, tasteless and sometimes fatal; the newspapers publish the annual toll. Most of the 21 victims who missed the rest of 1998 were senior citizens who were prevented from properly chewing the glutinous balls by false teeth.

**A PEASANT** woman boiling plums to make brandy in the Romanian village of Ruginoasa, died when the flames under her still set off a buried World War II shell. Her daughter was badly injured in the explosion. A similar fate awaited a drunk in Belgrade, Serbia, who tried to open a beer bottle with a live hand-grenade. It exploded in his face, killing him and injuring his drinking buddy and two passers-by.

**PIERRE POLESE**, 34, died at a family Christmas Eve feast in Monteban, France, after his wife put a hot dish on a glass table and it exploded, sending a flying shard into his throat.

**ANOTHER** home-brew fatality occurred just before Christmas 1993. Dimitru Dumitrazcu, 67, a farmer from Slatioara in Romania, was distilling brandy in his cellar when he was overcome by the fumes and fell into the barrel. He was dead when his wife found him.

**BOOZE** also affected the balance of brewery worker Boris Kalush, 34, who drowned after falling into a beer vat while trying to get a drink in Omsk, Siberia. Watchman Jorge Paz did the same while patrolling a brewery in Ponta Grossa, Brazil. And in Uganda, a distiller called Ntoni, who had been repeatedly warned not to drink the produce, went too far and after being seen at work "in an unusually good mood" went missing, only to be found dead by his partner, Florence, floating face down in a pool of hot amuna (brewing residue). Or at least that's what she said. Police, suspicious about Ntoni's quick burial, later arrested Florence and the local headman, who had approved his interment.

**AN AUSTRALIAN** woman of 77 froze to death in the top-opening food freezer at her house in the Sydney suburb of Punchbowl. She had apparently been leaning over the freezer when she overbalanced and hit her head. In Japan, businessman Oso Kantaki overbalanced too. He was trying to make the world's biggest jelly when he fell into the vast mould and drowned. In Aya Napa, Cyprus, British tourist Stephen Pepperell lost his balance as he tried to hurl a melon off his hotel balcony into a litter bin in the street and plunged two floors to his death. Pepperell was trying to show off his aim to his brother and two women who were also in the apartment.

**ON 17 MARCH 1996**, Julianna Farkas, aged 80, leaned over a sauerkraut barrel to scoop out a portion, fell in and drowned. Farkas, an ethnic Hungarian from Oradea in Romania, was visiting relations in Ebes, a village 100 miles east of Budapest. Neighbours discovered the accident when they heard the woman's three-year-old great-grandson crying in the yard with no one attending him. It was assumed that Farkas was overcome by the pungent cabbage fumes. The liquid in the barrel was 12in deep.

**ALSO SUPPOSEDLY** a fumes fatality, Mohammed Al-Assad was found dead in his bed, though we are not told where. "There were no marks whatsoever on his body," said the coroner, "but the autopsy revealed large amounts of methane gas in his system. Relatives have confirmed to me that his diet consisted principally of beans and cabbage, exactly the right combination of foods to produce large quantities of methane." A neighbour heard what he described as "the continuous sound of material being torn, followed by stifled screaming." It appeared that the man had repeatedly passed wind and fatally gassed himself in his small, air-tight bedroom. Three rescue workers broke down the door; all got sick and one had to be hospitalised. Appealing though this tale might be, it is, alas, almost certainly an urban legend.

**MORE LIKELY** was the death of three people in central Ukraine. Many people in the region rely on sugar beet, potatoes, cucumbers, onions and canned goods stored in cool cellars to carry them through the winter, but preservation is not always perfect. These three were killed by hydrogen sulphide fumes given off by rotting beet which had accumulated in the cellar, pushing out all the air.

**IN EGYPT**, a mother accidentally sprinkled rat poison instead of pepper on her 18-year-old daughter's lunch, killing the woman the day before her wedding. Um Hashem Abu Mahmoud died after suffering severe stomach pains. The family lived in Koum Hamada, 80 miles northwest of Cairo.

**HAVING** finished a speech to a toast-masters' club in Johannesburg in which he advised his audience to "enjoy life while you can, because death could strike at any moment," Danny du Toit, 49, collapsed and choked to death. Also offed by a very public choking was sideshow performer Stan Muller, who ate glass bottles for a living. He choked to death on one live on U.S. TV.

**IN WORTHING**, West Sussex, confused Harry Bush, 71, choked to death on his bath sponge. He has woken in the night feeling peckish in his nursing home and gone to look for something to eat, but mistook his sponge for food. He was found dead with two pieces of bitten-off sponge lodged in his throat. Louis Hutin, too, suffered a fatal snack urge in the middle of the night. He crept downstairs and opened the fridge, but the compressor exploded, killing him instantly.

**FRIDGE** opening is much more dangerous than most people appreciate. When Clinton R Doan of Idaho opened his, a beer keg ruptured, shot upwards and smashed into his head, killing him instantly. An exploding keg also took out city official Frans van der Vleuten in Heerlen, Holland. He was attaching a tap to one in preparation for a civic event when it ruptured explosively, blasting the lid upwards with tremendous force into his face.

**FIVE CHILDREN** died and another 150 people were taken ill after eating the flesh of a 40kg mystery, a turtle-like sea creature caught by a Vietnamese villager in the northern province of Quang Binh. One should clearly be careful what one eats; in the Philippines, three people died after eating a poisonous bullfrog as a snack with drinks. On Hainan Island, China, a food stall owner known for his special snake dishes was killed by two snakes he'd just beheaded. As he went to pick up the recently-severed heads, they sank their fangs into his hand and he died of the poisonous bites.

**KATHY TAGUE DI GIROLAMO**, 29, from Hatfield, Pennsylvania, didn't need to eat her food for it to kill her. She suffered from bronchial asthma and an allergy to shellfish. On 13 November 1994, she had trouble breathing after a waiter walked by her table with a steaming platter of shrimps. Her asthma inhaler was ineffective, her breathing worsened and, despite medical attention, her pulse rate plunged and her heart stopped. Such deaths merely from smelling certain foods are the result of a system-wide breakdown called anaphylactic shock and are exceedingly rare.

**HEINRICH GAMBACH**, of Munich, Germany, got nick-named 'The Cereal Killer' after murdering his wife. He got fed up with shredded wheat for breakfast every day for 10 years, so he rammed some down his wife Wilhemina's throat, choking her to death. "The night before I killed her, I told her I had to work 15 hours the next day and asked for a cooked breakfast. But the next morning she gave me shredded wheat as usual." He said: "I forced it down her throat. By the time I calmed down, she was dead." A more direct route was taken by barber Franco Delatrice. Fed up with his wife Maria, who served him green beans every night for three months, he shot her.

**JEAN-PAUL HENRY** was found dead at home nine months after he croaked. He was sprawled across four cases of wine on his living room floor, with 300 empty bottles on one side and 300 full ones on the other. Despite having lain there for such a long time – Henry was a recluse who had fallen out with his family – his body was perfectly preserved. He had consumed so much alcohol it had permeated all his tissues, causing him to mummify instead of decay.

# *Motorised Mayhem*

**Our love affair with the car is not daunted even by setbacks such as these.**

**ALEXANDRA GREER**, 13 months, strapped in a forward-facing child safety seat while being driven by her mother, Rebecca Blackman, in Boise, Idaho, was decapitated by a car airbag when the car collided with another vehicle at low speed. The child's head was blown out of a side window. Airbags inflate at up to 200mph and have been blamed for the deaths of at least 30 children.

**AN UN-NAMED** man drowned in a freak car accident in Los Angeles when his VW convertible smashed into a fire hydrant. Although his face was never submerged, water coming through the car roof hit his face with such force that he could not breathe. He was found dead in a car half-full of water.

**A GERMAN COUPLE** in their fifties took their old car to a scrapyard. They parked, completed the necessary paperwork and got back in the car to shelter from a sudden squall of rain. "The driver of the crane was told to process their car," said a police investigator. "He did so without realising that the couple were sitting inside again." The car was grabbed by the crane's steel claws and dropped in the crusher, which normally reduces cars to a small cube. It was stopped when the crane driver heard the woman's screams, but it was too late to save her husband. The crane driver was hospitalised for shock, but was expected to be charged with 'negligent manslaughter'.

**ARA ANANIAN**, a 32-year-old Québecois electronic engineer, was crushed by his 1984 manual Toyota Supra when he used the remote car starter and the car leapt forward. It was the first death by remote car starters, though the devices have caused problems in the past. A number of cars have smashed through garage doors in an outburst of high spirits and, in one case, the car started as soon as the owner's neighbours switched on their fan.

**MARY EIFRID**, 80, drove to her friend's house in Fort Wayne, Indiana, and as she drew up, fell out of her car. As she crawled towards the curb, the car turned 180 degrees, mounted the curb and pinned her underneath. Attempts to jack up the car failed.

**JAMES BURNS**'s truck developed an irritating noise, so Burns, of Alamo, Michigan, asked a friend to drive along the highway while he tried to work out the problem. His clothes got caught and he ended up "wrapped in the drive shaft" of his truck.

**IN HOLLAND**, a 72-year-old motorist hit a rabbit on the A6 motorway, north of Amsterdam. He pulled over at a motorway services exit and was walking back up the road to attend to the stricken animal when he was run over and killed by a car coming from the opposite direction.

**EDWARD MUSGROVE**, 32, attacked his estranged wife as she began an evening route as a Los Angeles bus driver. He grabbed the steering wheel, causing the bus to veer off the road, hit a tree and crash into a brick wall. The wife was not injured, but Musgrove was hurled through the windscreen into the wall and decapitated.

**DAVID MUSHIKELE**, 26, a Namibian, was struck and killed by a car just minutes after a bolt of lightning knocked him down in a street in Windhoek. Police were hunting the hit-and-run driver. Two other men were also hit by the lightning, but managed to stumble out of the car's path.

**AN ASIAN** taxi driver from Manchester tied one end of a rope around his neck and the other to a nearby lamppost, then drove off one early evening in December in his Toyota Carina. Security guards, investigating why the taxi was still there the following morning with its engine running, found the driver's head, still attached to the rope, a short distance away.

**HELMUT MEZER**, 18, from Austria, died in a high-speed car crash one week after getting his new driving licence and a BMW with the number plate DEAD1. The car skidded on a bend at 100mph, hit a bank and catapulted more than 200ft through the air before landing on its roof in a field. Mezer was killed instantly and a friend in the passenger seat was seriously injured.

**HELENA KADOW**, an 88-year-old Maryland woman, managed to write 'Help me' in lipstick before dying locked in her own car parked outside her home. Either mechanical failure – the car's windows and doors were electrically operated – or illness prevented her from getting out of the car and she died from the heat. Erik Peterson died from the cold. He pulled up outside his house in Denmark in freezing mid-winter temperatures and was found there the next day, dead in his seat, where a faulty seatbelt had pinned him until he froze to death.

**A WOMAN** died after the car in which she was a passenger hit a kangaroo on the Mitchell Highway, 55 miles west of Dubbo, New South Wales. The driver and another woman escaped unhurt.

**IN BIRMINGHAM**, a freak accident killed a woman pedestrian. Jason Richards, 22, was driving his E-registration Ford Escort when the axle snapped, sending the back wheel and the axle stub careering 400 yards down the next road. Cars swerved to avoid the hurtling tyre and metal, but Jean Bray, 58, took the full force of it as it smashed into her, sending her sprawling on the pavement. She died later in hospital. A West Midlands police spokesman said it was a tragic accident: "I have only ever heard of this happening once before when a wheel came off a lorry."

**A BRITISH TOURIST** also died in a freak accident caused by a chain-reaction road crash. Albert Smeaton was sitting by the road eating a watermelon with his wife when a sheet of metal blew off a passing lorry. It missed Albert completely, but forced a car to swerve and crash into a street sign. The sign then toppled and it was this that struck Albert on the head and killed him.

**JOANNE BERGESON** of Santa Clara, California, died in an even more surprising accident on the freeway near San Francisco International Airport. Her passenger said they were driving along Highway 101 when a car jack "suddenly appeared in the air." It smashed through Bergeson's car windscreen. She died of head injuries an hour and a half later.

**TWO TRUCKERS** in South Korea got out of their cabs in the middle of a Seoul motorway to argue about a collision and were mown down and killed by a bus.

**TINA PARKER** and her eight-year-old daughter Jennifer were killed when their car collided with an asphalt lorry which had gone out of control after its brakes failed. It wasn't the collision that killed them: it was the asphalt. The truck dumped tons of it onto their car, burying it completely in molten tarmac. Tina was dead when firemen dug her out and Jennifer died later in hospital.

**IN BUENOS AIRES**, travellers on a bus were delayed for more than seven hours when the driver pulled over to the side of the road and apparently went to sleep. After a while, an irate passenger got up to shake him awake ... and discovered he'd dropped dead. A couple of months earlier, another Buenos Aires bus driver had criss-crossed the city for 12 hours with a dead man sitting four seats behind him without anyone noticing. And if you were beginning to think this was a purely Argentinian phenomenon, Fumio Sudo, who died of a heart attack on a Tokyo underground train, went unnoticed for five hours, completing three circuits of the tube network before anyone realised he was a corpse. One commuter who saw him said: "I thought he was asleep. The underground is one of the few places we Japanese get to relax."

**TWO TRAFFIC WARDENS** in Bologna, Italy ended up under investigation for possible manslaughter charges after they wrote out a ticket for a van without noticing that the driver was dying inside. Traffic wardens seem good at this. Ten days after he disappeared police in Charlottesville discovered the body of Lyle O. Walker, 41, in the back of his van in a city parking lot, He had been shot in the back of the head with a small-calibre pistol. For several days traffic control officers had been sticking tickets to the van's windscreen, but it was only when a fifth ticket was being dished out that police were called to investigate the van and found Mr Walker decomposing inside.

# *Long Pork*

**Most things, apparently, taste like chicken:
we taste like pork.**

**TWO UKRAINIAN** brothers were convicted of beating up a
homeless man and beheading him with an axe. They cut some
flesh from the corpse which they fried and ate. The head was
displayed in the flat as a trophy. Anatoloy Novikov was sentenced to death and his brother Andriy sent down for 10 years.

**ILSHAT KUZIKOV**, 35, was seized in his one-room flat at 22
Ordzhonikidze Street, St Petersburg, on 23 August 1995 after
the severed heads of Misha Bochkov and Edik Vassilevsy had
been found in nearby streets. There were two legs and arms in
the hall and a casserole by the oven containing human bones,
picked clean. A plastic bag hanging outside the window was
filled with marinated human flesh and onions. A shopping bag
contained dried human ears and other parts, and there were
many jars of pickled flesh, which police referred to as "winter
supplies." Kuzilov, a diagnosed schizophrenic who had been in
and out of mental institutions, offered the investigators human

meat and vodka if they let him go. He kept saying things like: "Ever tried human liver? It's really tasty."

**SEEMINGLY AGREEING** with him were Aleksandr Maslich 23, and Aleksei Goluzov, 25, prisoners in Rubtsovsk in the Alta region of Siberia. They strangled another inmate aged 23, cut out his organs, cooked them in a washbowl held over a blazing blanket and then ate them "to add some spice to their life." Maslich was inside for an earlier triple murder; he had been sentenced to death the previous year. Goluzov, inside for robbery, got another 15 years. Both were declared sane. In May 1996, Maslich had also strangled his murderer cellmate with a blanket, cut out his liver and was caught trying to boil it over a fire made of rubber piping from a tap.

**POLICE** in Sebastopol, in the Crimea, entering the home of a former convict, found the mutilated remains of bodies being prepared for eating. The flat's owner, her mother and her boyfriend had been stabbed to death and their bodies neatly butchered. The internal organs of two victims were in saucepans and nearby there was a plate of freshly-roasted pieces of flesh.

**YELENA DALNOVA**, 76, was arrested on suspicion of killing her husband, then eating and canning his remains. Neighbours found the partial remains of Nikolai Dalonov, 83, on the stairs near the couple's apartment in Kaliningrad, outside Moscow. Cans of human flesh were found in the Dalonovas's fridge. Going a step further was Gulnara Hinz, who took a distinctly Shakespearean approach to cannibalism. She stabbed her violent husband to death, baked his flesh in the oven and served it to members of his family at his birthday party in Uzbekistan. When relatives asked where he was, the 26-year-old woman told them they had just eaten him.

**A MAN** in the Siberian town of Kemerovo confessed to killing a well-known criminal, Vladimir Laptin, and using his flesh as the filling for pelmeni, a Russian version of ravioli, which he shared with two drinking companions. The crime came to light after some tramps found the victim's head on a dump. Around the same time, a man was found frying human flesh in a house in the southern Russian city of Krasnodar. The dismembered bodies of two elderly men were found in the bathroom.

**A CANNIBAL** who ate his son and a drinking companion was committed to an asylum by a court in the Tula region of Moscow in March 1996. The previous autumn, a man was arrested in the centre of Tula after biting the throat of a passer-by.

**A MAN** of 36 was hospitalised after stabbing his 57-year-old mother to death, eating her entrails and jumping out of the fourth-floor window of their apartment in Moscow. He told police he was enraged by his mother's cursing government policies. After killing her, he carved up the body, ran some of her entrails through a meat grinder and ate them while watching television. He jumped several hours later, suffering concussion, a broken spine and numerous cuts and bruises. And just to prove this sort of thing isn't confined to Russia, Henry Heepe, 50, from Akron, Ohio, was arrested for allegedly killing his mother, then cooking and eating parts of her.

**LIVESTOCK SPECIALIST** Sergei Golovkin was sentenced to death by a Moscow court after being convicted of abusing, murdering and eating 11 boys. Golovkin lured his victims from children's camps to his home and over an eight-year period, tortured two or three at a time in his garage. He then buried the bodies in a nearby wood with heads, arms and genitals cut off.

**A GANG** of six South Korean cannibals with a grudge against the rich planned and carried out a unique terror campaign against the customers of a top Seoul department store. They had a list of 1,200 of them and planned to kill and eat their way through the lot. They had murdered, cooked and eaten at least five of them by the time police caught up with them.

**ANTHROPOLOGIST** Lucas Solomon, studying the tribes in Lae, Papua New Guinea, came across a man named Czi-Czi Lugora, who had reputedly eaten more friends than hot dinners. Lugora claimed to have eaten more than 500 people over 21 years and Solomon said: "He's the most feared and respected man ever."

# *Number One in a Field of One*

**There arc always some demises which defy classification!**

**AN EGYPTIAN** searching for the treasures of the pharaohs was found on 5 July sitting cross-legged on top of a mountain, his corpse pecked by crows. Police in southern Egypt were searching the area near Saqolta Mountain in Sohag province for four of his relatives, who accompanied him on the treasure hunt.

**IAN GAMBLE**, 16, was stabbed to death on 24 February 1996 after an argument with some youths as he walked through the grounds of Barnard Castle, Co Durham. A few yards away was a memorial to his brother Darren, who was killed in an accident in March 1988, also at the age of 16. Darren and his friend Steven Laybourn had been sitting in a car in the garage of Steven's home with the engine running to keep warm; but they fell asleep and were killed by the exhaust fumes.

**SEVERAL** French World War I veterans died of joy after hearing they were to receive the Legion of Honour to mark the 77th anniversary of the war's end, according to the veterans' affairs minister. He said he knew of at least two who died filling in the form to receive it.

**PIERRE PERDOT,** 48, died of a bullet wound, 21 years after being shot in Nice, France. His former wife, Marie, who shot him in 1974, was charged with murder.

**A BOY** of nine died six hours after being bitten by a rabid dog in Bucharest. He was the second child to die of rabies in 1996 in Romania, where thousands of stray dogs roam the capital. The cases are thought to be the first rabies deaths in Europe for over a decade.

**SOUTH AFRICAN** taxidermist Roelf Uys was celebrating his 33rd birthday in the bush in Northern Province when a hunter saw his hat bobbing in the long grass and, mistaking it for a pheasant, shot him dead.

**PROSPERO** Capellar Barrios, 46, a Venezuelan ice cream seller, was killed on 16 September 1997 when a cast-iron lamppost crashed down on the spot where he had worked for more than 14 years. Thieves had removed its retaining screws. Barrios died of head wounds in the colonial centre of Caracas before medical help could arrive.

**MIGUEL FARADO** was woken by what he thought was a burglar in his Miami home. He grabbed his semi-automatic, went to investigate, fired one shot and killed his pregnant 24-year-old wife Mabel with a bullet through the head.

**FIFTY-ONE** people were killed when a train smashed into another train which had halted after hitting a stray goat in fog near Lucknow.

**NORFOLK** teenager Kim Whiter came home from school to find that her father Keith had committed suicide in the garage. She rang her mother Jacqueline, who immediately left Felixstowe to comfort her daughter. During the trip, the BMW in which she was a passenger hit a tree and burst into flames, killing her too.

**LAURA KUCERA**, 20, survived four days in a ditch after being shot by her ex-boyfriend. He shot her twice in the head and once in the shoulder, then left her for dead in a remote area. He later had second thoughts and led rescuers to her. Doctors were amazed to find she'd survived despite her injuries and four days in near-freezing temperatures clad only in a T-shirt and shorts. She spent 51 days in hospital and painfully relearned how to walk and use her arms. Just under a year later, her fatal relationship with ditches reasserted itself when her car ran off the road as she drove to her grandmother's, killing her instantly.

**DANIEL JONES**, 21, dug an 8-ft hole on Buxton beach, North Carolina, and settled down in his deckchair, well protected from the wind. The walls of his hole collapsed and it took rescuers with heavy equipment, egged on by 200 spectators, an hour to free him. He was declared dead when he reached hospital.

WHILE playing in a park in Lorca, Spain, a young girl found a box filled with more than 30 human eyeballs. Police were baffled.

A DRIVER who bought a bargain car at a New York car auction got an optional extra that doesn't come with most vehicles: when he opened the trunk, he found the handcuffed corpse of a woman in it. The motor had been on the auction lot for three months.

ALSO finding bodies in profusion is Gheorghe Cassas, known to colleagues as 'The Cadaver Cabby'. A New York cab driver for more than 13 years, over a three-year period Gheorghe discovered five bodies and six severed heads. He has turned up various shooting victims, plus three children who died jumping from a burning building. The six heads were in a cardboard box mislaid by a doctor from the New York Eye and Ear Infirmary. "This never happened in Romania," Cassas lamented: "There, nobody uses the drugs, the guns, the knives. New York is a crazy city."

ACCORDING to Reuters, twice in five months during 1994 German tourists unknowingly spent the night in a motel room that contained a rotting corpse. In March that year, a maid at the Travellers Hotel near Miami airport found a decaying female corpse under the mattress in a room occupied by a German visitor after he complained of the smell. Then in August the manager of the Venice Hotel in Fort Lauderdale found a rotting male body wrapped in a plastic bag along with air fresheners stuffed under a bed when clearing up after a German family. The Germans had only stayed for one night and the fly-covered bag had clearly been there longer, so they were clearly not involved and had not noticed the room's extra occupant during their stay. If these stories were not so detailed, we would suspect they were manifestations of a recurrent urban legend.

**A BIZARRE** killer left parts of his victim, sometimes spray-painted lurid colours, in a grotesque trail around public places in New Mexico. Arms and legs were found in boxes and wrapped in blankets, the torso appeared beside a highway in Chapparal and the head turned up in a box outside someone's apartment. Police said they were all parts of an unidentified woman.

**SAN FRANCISCO** experienced a massive influx of Chinese immigrants, most of them dead, in the run-up to Hong Kong's reversion to Chinese rule. The city has the West's largest Chinese population and it used to be traditional to ship the deceased back to China for burial in home ground. However, with Hong Kong coming under the rule of Beijing, its residents worried that the authorities might build roads or offices over graveyards as they have in other Chinese cities, so they exhumed their ancestors and shipped them to the States for reburial in San Francisco's cemetery district, Colma. There a 13.5-acre graveyard constructed and landscaped in accordance with feng-shui principles, was opened in 1993 to accommodate the Chinese dead.

**IN FINLAND**, authorities dread midsummer eve, as the entire population goes wild with celebration, taking a three-day holiday for drinking and dancing. About 30 generally die: "Last year it was 27," said Petri Lepannen of the National Safety Board. "Fourteen drowned, six died in road accidents, two were suicides, a family of three burned to death in their cottage, a woman walked in front of a train and a Swede jumped off a ferry to rescue his mobile phone. Plus a few stabbings. But it was a wet weekend – that helped." Juha Pekka Korkeila of the University of Tampere, who has studied midsummer madness, said: "The contrast with winter is so extreme people lose their grip." Sari Uihtonen, 26, a student who lost an uncle and two classmates to midsummer excess, commented: "Midsummer is a tragedy for families, but it's a truly Finnish way to go."

**HU PAO-YIN**, 35, stabbed her mother-in-law to death on Christmas Eve. Her reason for this, she told police, was that "I am the most beautiful woman in the world and the existence of other women is unnecessary." Her adoptive mother survived a similar attack.

**BHUPENDRA PAUDAL** from Kanyam in Nepal, who claimed that he had been given heavenly powers by the god Siva, killed his wife in front of his family because she was not as beautiful as the goddess Parvati, consort of Lord Siva. He reasoned that this sacrifice would help his wife to become as beautiful as Parvati. It didn't.

**ANGIE JERSTON**, of Denver, Colorado, was touching up her lipstick as she drove to work when she was forced to brake sharply. The tube shot into her mouth and stuck in her windpipe. She died because she had locked the doors for safety and rescuers were unable to get in. A year and a half later, the *Daily Record* reported that another woman driver in Denver choked to death when she swallowed her lipstick. Police said she was doing her make-up when she braked suddenly. Either Denver is a very dangerous place to do your lipstick, or someone is recycling the news.

# CHAPTER EIGHTEEN

# *Final Fiascos*

**Ideally, when the end comes, we'd all like to die with dignity. Fate, however, often has other ideas.**

**A 32-YEAR-OLD** German died when a camp-site lavatory exploded as he tried to light a cigarette, blasting him through a closed window. Police in Montabaur, south of Bonn, said the explosion appeared to have been caused by leaking gas from the septic tank or a defective natural gas pipe.

**IN ACCRA**, Ghana, Theophilous Kouame Gakpo, 23, was in too much of a hurry to queue for the public toilets, so he enlisted two of his friends to go round the back with him and lever the lid off the septic tank. He then squatted down to relieve himself over the edge, but slipped on ground muddy after heavy rain and toppled into the pit. Municipal officials were called and rushed to the scene to empty the tank, but failed to find the man's body. Perhaps he'd just climbed out?

**GLEN PELMEAR**, 33, was electrocuted while sitting on a public lavatory at Ryde harbour on the Isle of Wight. A broken light fitting had made the whole row of all-metal cubicles 'live'. Police found the body with sparks still showering from it. They initially announced that vandals had tampered with the wiring and if caught would be charged with manslaughter; later they said it was an accident.

**SANOON THAMMAKAI**, a 47-year-old Thai villager, had a heart attack when his electricity bill arrived. Usually the bill hovered around 200 baht; this time, it was for 19,249 baht. He was dead by the time he reached hospital.

**TODDLER** Megan Barosa, aged three, was killed when children switched on a fire-hydrant in New York. The torrent of water which hosed out of the hydrant ripped the child from her carer's arms and hurled her into the path of an oncoming dust-cart, which ran over her.

**WHEN** a two-year-old boy died of smoke inhalation during a fire at his home in Lewisham, his remains were taken to Greenwich Mortuary, where a post-mortem was carried out. Several weeks later a second post-mortem was required, but pathologists were horrified to discover that in the interim, the tot's lungs had vanished. They called in Southwark Criminal Investigation Department who investigated allegations of organ theft, but were unable to find out what had happened to the lungs. In a statement they said: "We investigated an allegation of theft of organs.... It has not been proven that the organs were not taken ... it could be there was some kind of hospital error. It is just not possible to say what happened."

**TRAGIC TOT** Carlos Merino, from Pamplona, was playing with matches and set light to his mattress. As the flames took hold, the terrified three-year-old hid in the wardrobe. Firefighters burst into the bedroom and used the wardrobe to smash the windows of the smoke-filled room. It was nor certain whether Carlos, whose leg was still in plaster from a previous calamity, had died from smoke inhalation or defenestration.

**NICOTINE** addict Ray King, 62, decided to have a final smoke the night before he was duc to go into hospital for cancer treatment. He was too weak to get out of bed when the bedclothes caught light and was found the next morning beside his still-smouldering blankets, dead from smoke inhalation.

**BRYAN BORSA**, 21, visited a friend's apartment and for some reason cleaned a loaded SKS assault rifle. It accidentally discharged and the bullet went through the ceiling of his friend's apartment, through the chest of his upstairs neighbour, Richard Brockway (who was having a quiet Saturday night on his sofa), and embedded itself in the ceiling.

**A GUM-CHEWING** motorist was killed after he blew a giant bubble which burst and stuck to his glasses, blinding him. Abner Kriller, of Albany, Australia, ran his car off the road and plunged down a hill.

**AN 80-YEAR-OLD** pensioner went into bushes to spend a penny at the edge of a cliff at St Gilgen, Austria. The ground gave way and she plunged hundreds of feet to her death. A week later, Japanese professor Seitaro Takayama, 68, stepped back on a cliff top at St Just, Cornwall, and fell 40ft to his death.

**KARATE** brown belt and Thai boxing enthusiast Scott Kell, 23, lost his balance doing high kicks and plunged to his death through an open window on the 10th floor of a tower block.

**POLLY PERRY**, 54, decided to make a parachute jump to help overcome her fear of heights but died on her first attempt. She was harnessed to an instructor during a tandem jump at Santa Fe, New Mexico, and they fell 8,500 feet to their deaths when the main parachute failed to open. A similar fate awaited Tess Elliot, 23, then the reigning Miss North Carolina, who took up parachuting to cure her acrophobia. She fell to her death when her chute's cords tangled.

**AN ELDERLY THAI** woman was watching TV with her family when a parachutist landed on her. His chute had failed to open and he had plummeted 10,000ft before crashing through the roof of her house in Ubon Ratchathani. Both died instantly. Also in Thailand, a young Danish woman died while sunbathing by a pool in Bangkok when a man fell from the 18th floor of a high-rise condominium and landed on her. The man also died. It happens in Brazil as well. There a woman died of shock when a body slammed into the ground next to her after a mid-air collision between two light aircraft.

**GEORGE PEARCE**, 61, died when his VW was crushed under 20 tons of pork. Fire crews unloaded the overturned lorry but were far too late. A retired miner, who never had an accident underground, died when tons of coal buried him in his own backyard in the former mining village of Nelson in Glamorgan. Tom Gray, 86, was getting fuel from his bunker when a wall collapsed.

**SUN TIESHAN**, of Xinjiang, China, dropped a bucket down a 9-metre well while he was drawing water. Sun's neighbour tried to get it back but the rope he was using broke and he had to be rescued by Sun's son, who became trapped. Sun then fell in, followed shortly afterwards by his grandson. By the time the fire department arrived, grandfather, son and grandson were all dead. When 25-year-old Jordanian Qassem Saleh lost his car keys, he and his companions thought they might have fallen down a nearby well. Attached to a rope, Saleh descended the 33-foot shaft, but suffocated from lack of oxygen. His brothers succumbed when they tried to rescue him, as did the friends who tried to rescue the brothers. A sixth man survived.

**DETECTIVE-SERGEANT** Daniel Edwards, 40, was found on 30 August 1997 trapped between a tree and his patrol car on a road between Muizenberg and Fish Hoek near Cape Town in South Africa. Captain Jacques Wiese said it appeared that Sgt Edwards had parked his vehicle on a slope when he went to relieve himself. It had then rolled down the embankment and crushed him.

**WHEN** 36-stone Patricia Mullen, 31, died in Chicago, police called to remove the body made crude remarks about her size and left her naked corpse on public view. Needless to say, her family sued.

**THE BODY** of Egeneh Bishara was supposed to be flown from Paris to Tel Aviv for burial. Some of her family flew on the same plane to accompany her corpse, but when they arrived, the airline could find no trace of the coffin. Air France admitted they did not know what had happened to the body. They got sued too. Christopher Walsh also went astray in transit. An urn containing his remains was handed in to the lost property office at Fenchurch Street station in London after they had been discovered in the ladies' toilet. At the time of the report no one had come forward to claim them. Perhaps he was having a final wish fulfilled?

IN NEW JERSEY, the *Passaic Herald* noted the following: "The medical examiner's office filed a report based on clinical observation, that listed the cause of death as pneumonitis or a bad cold, but an autopsy found Mr Acevedo had died of multiple gunshot wounds to the head."

PARENTS Tom and Tami DeBlois, of Readsboro, Vermont, caused problems with their memorial to baby daughter Jonica Deanna, who had died in a car accident. They started out by placing a laminated picture of the child on her gravestone, but then added to it a variety of other items. Embellishments included a knee-high ceramic doll; a pink lamb; two flower boxes; a small tree upon which ornaments are hung at Christmas; a crouching lion; a painted racoon; a ceramic rabbit; and a wooden carving of Jonica on a swing. When they erected a trellis over the gravestone, the cemetery's board of commissioners decided things had gone too far and insisted the display was taken down. The grave "looks like a circus." one said. The DeBlois removed the trellis in a spirit of compromise. In Barcelona, too, public officials did not entirely appreciate someone's idea of a memorial. A judge intervened to prevent Maria Oridalo, 62, having a handbag made from her late husband's skin.

# References

# REFERENCES

## CHAPTER 1: I'LL GET OUT OF THIS IF IT KILLS ME!

Flying moon *D.Mirror* 24 Jun 1995. Lift lovers *D.Record* 4 Oct 1995. Half-Nelson *News Tribune (WA)*, 23 Sept 1997, *[R]* 3 Aug 1995, *Newport & Olney Citizen*, 26 June 1997 *Huddersfield Daily Examiner*, 26 Feb 1997. Pasta peril *People*, 28 Aug; *New York Post*, 27 Oct 1994. Mixer mangling *Sun* 28 Mar? Deadly display *D.Mail*, 23 Aug 1997. Vat's it *[R]* 23 Jan 1997, *Rocky Mountain News*, 10 Sept 1994, *Independent*, 7 Sept 1995, *Guardian*, 12 Sept 1995. Mangone *Nottingham Evening Post*, 8 Sept 1995. Computer fall *D.Record*, 18 April; *People*, 28 April 1996. Accountancy overdose *[R]* 3 Dec 1997. Revenge, served cold *[AP]* 25 July 1997. Dung blast *[AFP]* 5 April 1998. Blacksmith surprise *N & O Times*, 11 Mar 1997. Lawnmower death *N & O Times*, 11 Mar 1997. Rollered *Electronic Telegraph*, 28 November 1996, *D.Record*, 20 Oct 1992. Death stripe *D.Record* 20 Sept 1994. Ladder crash *Western Mail* 22 Feb 1995. Couldn't hit a barn door *Guardian* 3 Feb 1998. Brush with death *D.Star* 9 Sept 1994. Rock'n'roll *Guardian* 12 Sept 1996. Telescopic *D.Telegraph* 2 May 1987. Armoured attack *D.Star* 4 Feb 1994.

## CHAPTER 2: FATAL COINCIDENCE

Blowhole *Nando Times*, 11 Apr 1997. Mind the bullocks! *D.Express* 2 Oct 1982. Two bikers *Sun* 9 Apr 1986. Twin tankers *D.Telegraph*, 2 Mar 1996. Deadly dealings *D.Telegraph*, 6 Dec 1997. *Wolverhampton Express & Star*, 18 Oct 1994; *S.Times*, 7 July 1996. Smash Hit *Time*, 18 Mar 1996. The name's the same *D.Mail*, 25 Oct 1995. Birthdays *Newark (NJ) Star Ledger*, 5 April 1997. Champagne supertanker *S.Express* 15 Jun 1980. I'm back! *Sydney Morning Herald* 29 Nov 1995. Camcorder fall *D.Star* 24 Aug 1993. Postfall *Wolverhampton Express & Star* 3 Apr 1995. M*A*S*Hed *Victoria (BC) Times-Colonist* 25 Feb 1996.

## CHAPTER 3: LOVE 'N' MARRIAGE

Elbow job *S.Mail*, 28 April 1996. Going together *Times*, 10 Aug 1996, *York Post*, 28 Jan 1998. Hiccup horror *[AP]* 16 Jan 1997, *[AP]* 17 Nov 1997. Nailed *Scotsman*, 18 July; *D.Star*, 19 July; *S.Sport*, *People*, 20 July 1997. On the hop *News of the World*, 15 Feb 1998, *S.Express* 5 Mar 1995. 13 year delay *S.Mail*, 24 Dec 1995, *Times*, 14 Feb 1995. Getting the drop *D.Telegraph*, 14 July 1997. Hairy *Hong Kong Standard*, 9 Sept 1997. Family fallout *Guardian*, 15 Jan 1998. Interfering git *Independent*, 7 Mar 1997. How not to commit the perfect murder *Washington Post* 25 + 26 Sept 1993. Exit sign *Edinburgh Eve. News*, 9 July 1996. Final blow *Sydney D.Telegraph*, 3 Oct 1997. Fatal Lewinsky *Sun* 6 Oct 1995. Fatal fornications *D.Record* 3 Sept 1993, *Western Mail* 17 Jan 1995. Choose death *[AP]* 29 Oct 1996.

## CHAPTER 4: GOD HAVE MERCY

Hot baptism *The Globe & Mail*, 30 June 1994. Priestly heart attacks *EDP* 9 Jun 1995, *Sussex Eve. Argus* 14 Nov 1994. Buried alive *Independent*, 21 Mar 1998. Zapped to heaven *Yorkshire Post*, 1 Mar 1997. Haj horror *[AP]* 9 April 1998. Hindu horrors *Eastern Evening News*, 15 July; *Halifax Evening Courier*, 16 July 1996, *[R]* 28 Aug 1996. Divine ingratititude *Ghana Daily Graphic*, 3 May 1996, *Hong Kong Eastern Express*, 20 Jan 1996. In the name of Allah *[AFP]* 7 May 1997. Limpopo lunacy *Times*, *D.Telegraph*, 15 Jan 1998, *Sun* 28 Jan 1995. Fortune runs out *D.Mirror* 18 Feb 1986, *Newcastle Eve. Chronicle* 13 Oct 1995. The world doesn't end (again) *[AP]* 3+4 Jan 1996. Fatal virgin *Victoria (BC) Times-Colonist* 12 Jul 1994. Elephant end *Church Times*, 16 May 1997. Holy rockets *[R]* 3 June 1997. The Lewes horror *News of the World*, 28 April; *Times*, 13 June; *Sunday Mirror*, 7 July 1996. Satanic poisoning *D.News* 12 Apr 1998.

## CHAPTER 5: THAT'S ENTERTAINMENT, OR AT LEAST IT WAS

Splashed Elvis *Observer* 30 Jun 1996. Meeting his nemesis *D.Telegraph*, 16 July 1994, *Western Morning News*, 21 Mar 1996. Balloonacy *People*, 26 Oct 1997. Fatal spring *D.Telegraph* 26 Aug 1998. Exotic gunwoman *S.Express* 26 Nov 1995. Suffocated stripper *D.Record*,30 Aug 1997. Daredevils die *Weekend* 23–29 Apr 1990 *S.Mail* 16 Jun 1996. Stars stiff *Guardian* 13 Sept 1996, *South London Press*, 27 Aug 1997, *D.Star* 28 Sept 1994. Tiger feat *[AP]* 9 May; *D.Telegraph*, 26 May 1997. Hang-ups *Victoria (BC) Times-Colonist*, 29 Oct 1994, 2 Nov 1988, 30 Oct 1988, 25 Oct 1990, *[AP]* 15 May 1996. Another dangler *[R]*, *D.Telegraph*, 19 Aug 1997. Operatic exit *[AP]* 5 Jan; *New York Post*, 6 Jan 1996. Country death songs *Guardian* 12 Sept 1996. Alas, poor Jonathan *Toronto Globe Mail* 6 Mar 1995. Erased *Guardian*, 14 Jan 1997, *Independent*, 21 Feb 1995, *D.Telegraph*, 9 Aug 1995. Stiff competition *D.Sport* 13 Oct 1994.

## CHAPTER 6: HOMES AND GARDENS

Boiled *D.Mirror*, 22 June 1994. Brush with death *D.Record*, 15 July 1995. Papered S. *Express*, 23 April 1995. Telly topple *[AFP]* 9 Jan 1996. Paranoid Pole *[R]* 20 Nov 1996, *S.Mail* (Scotland), 12 June; *Europa Times*, April 1994, *S.People* 10 Nov 1985. Dishwasher death *Guardian*, *D.Telegraph*, *Mirror*, 2 April 1997, *D.Mail*, 14 May 1994. Sucker tub *D.Record* 29 May 1996, *S.Telegraph* 10 Dec 1995. Front room drowning *Sun* 9 Mar 1995. Loathsome landlord *D.Telegraph* 15 Jan 1987. Jammed junk-fiend *S.Times*, 2 Feb 1997, *D.Telegraph*, 4 Mar 1997, *D.Mirror* 24 Oct 1996. Basement body *New York Daily News*, 2+4 Dec; *BT (Denmark)*, 4 Dec 1994. An oak with her name on *Mirror*, 4 July 1997. Shower shock *D.Telegraph*, 25 Sept 1997, *Guardian* 25 Aug 1994. Lawnmower death *[AP]* 1 June 1997. Everybody needs good neighbours *Victoria (BC) Times-Colonist* 7 Aug 1996, *S.Mail* 24 Apr 1994, *USA Today* 2 Nov 1994. Toppings *Middlesborough Eve.Gazette*, 31 Mar 1998, *D.Mirror* 14 Jan 1994.

## CHAPTER 7: MISJUDGING MACHINES

Beheaded *[AP]* 7 Jan 1995. Escalation *Victoria BC Times-Colonist*, 18 Sept 1987, *[AP]*, 13 Mar 1997. The train strikes twice *D.Telegraph*, 10 Aug 1995, *La Repubblica (Italy)*, 9 Nov; *D.Telegraph*, 10 Nov 1995. 70 Years late *[AP]* 16 Jan 1996. Runaway car *The S.Record (Hackensack, NJ)*, 6 Nov, 1994. Swipe 'n'fry *[AP]*, 28 June 1995. Live line licker *Nottingham Eve. Post* 6 Sept 1996. Tamagotcha *[R]* 8 April 1998. His biggest fan *D.Record*, *D.Star*, 9 Jan 1995. Second try *Times*, *D.Express*, 23 Feb 1996. Fatal get-well *S.Express* 3 June 1979. Raining men *New York Post*, *Houston (TX) Chronicle*, 24 May; *New York Daily News*, 25 May 1996. Bridgehead *[R]* 25 Feb 1995. Snowmobile snuff *[AP]* 20 Feb 1996. Radio blast *D.Star* 22 Feb 1994. No fishkill *[AP]* 17 Jun 1998. No Lift *North Bay (Ontario) Nugget* 9 May 1998. Fried baby *NY D News* 27 Aug 1993. Train trouble *Sun* 4 Apr 1996.

## CHAPTER 8: BEGINNINGS, MIDDLES AND ENDS

Smartarse *S.Mail* 22 Aug 1993. Camel bloke *D.Telegraph* 14 Apr 1995, *[R]* 27 Dec 1995, *D.Mail*, 27 Nov 1995. Marriage dead *Sussex Eve. Argus* 11 Oct 1994, *Halifax Eve.Courier* 21 Oct 1994, *D.Record* 20 Mar 1995. Menu misery *National (Romania)*, 14 Nov 1997. Vase marrying *D.Record* 26 Oct 1996. Fast switch *D.Record* 28 Oct 1996. Morbid couture *D.Record* 30 Oct 1995. Leg end *D.Record* 7 Nov 1994. Jehovah's witless *D.Telegraph*, 25 Jan 1996. Dead digger *Adelaide Advertiser* 16 July 1996, *D.Mirror*, 4 Sept 1996. Crushed *D.Record* 2 May 1995. OD *Eastern Eve. News*, 11 July 1996. Hearse smash *S.Mail* 24 Dec 1995. Hearse horror *D.Telegraph* 1 Dec 1994. Let me out! *News of the World*, 16 Mar 1997. *[AFP]* 21 Aug 1997. Ash scrap *Middlesborough Eve. Gazette* 22 Apr 1998. Ash splash *[AP]* 3 Feb 1995. Ash stray *D.Mirror* 5 Oct 1996, *The Record (Hackensack, NJ)* 6 Sept 1996. Stiff stack *USA Today* 13 Oct 1994, *D.Record* 27 Sept 1995, *D.Sport* 2 Dec 1994, *S.Mail* 11 Nov

1995. Fatal first act *Independent on Sunday* 3 Mar 1996. Mystery bones *Boston Mass. Herald* 11 May 1996. Dead neighbourly *Birmingham Post* 8 Jun 1996.

## CHAPTER 9: MEDICAL MASSACRE

Exploding bed *Mirror*, 10 Sept 1997. Exploding patients *Western Mail*, 22 April 1997, *Sun*, 7 Mar 1998. *Edinburgh Evening News*, 10 Aug 1994. Hot bath *Edinburgh Evening News*, 10 Aug 1994, *Philadelphia Inquirer*, 16 Nov 1996. Unplugged *D.Record*, 7 Mar 1998, *[AP]*, 26 Aug 1997. Choker *Salt Lake (UT) Tribune*, 15 Sept 1997, *D.Star*, 5 May; *S. Mail*, 15 May 1994. OOP tooth *Guardian*, *D.Telegraph*, *Mirror*, 29 July 1997. Over-excited *D Record*, 9 Feb 1996. Not bypassed *Daily Post*, 9 Feb 1996. Feeling liftless *The People*, 31 Oct 1993. Chopper chopper chopped *South China Morning Post*, 14 Oct 1996. Aphrodeathiac *[AP]* 25 Nov 1995. Overconfident! *[AFP]* 9 Dec 1995. New head *Hong Kong Eastern Express*, 7 May 1996. Tampon trouble Devilish period *South China Morning Post*, 8 Dec 1996. Drastic ant remedy *D.Record*, 30 Sept; *Middle East Times*, Dec 1996. DIY dentists *[R]* 9 Sept 1995, *South China Morning Post*, 27 April 1996. Insulin end *Western D.Press*, 3 July 1996. Potato death *Times*, *D.Telegraph*, *D.Mail*, *Mirror*, 19 April 1997. Embolism *D.Mail*, *D.Telegraph*, 4 July 1997. No train *Wolverhampton Expresss & Star*, 17 May 1995. Dry drowning *D.Record*, 23 Feb 1994. Cursed playground *Eve. Standard (London)*, 15 Jan 1998. Contamination panic *D.Telegraph* 16 May 1998. Wired gland *Scots Law Times via Glasgow Herald* 9 Mar 1995.

## CHAPTER 10: THIS SPORTING LIFE

Fatal trout *News of the World*, 5 April 1998. Bear battle *[AP]* 7 Nov 1997, *S.Express*, 10 Dec 1995. Baited badger *[AFP]* 11 Oct 1997. Posthumous deer revenge *Victoria (BC) Times-Colonist*, 7 Nov 1994. Marlin catches man *D.Mail*, 20 June 1994. Fried not poached *Birmingham Mail*, 5 May 1995, *D.Record*, 16 June 1994. Fiji three *[R]* 16 Jan, 17 Feb 1995. Fijian fish fight back *[R]* 25 May 1995, *Wolverhampton Express & Star*, 15 Mar; *D.Express*, 16 Mar 1996. Caught on his own hook *D.Mail*, 17 Mar 1998. Golf rat *D.Mirror*, 30 Aug 1996. Shafted *[AP]* 12 July 1994, *D.Mirror* 4 Aug 1993, *D.Telegraph* 7 Aug 1993. Golf diver *S.Express*, 14 May; *D.Mirror*, 19 May 1995. Fatal stroke *S.Express* 19 Mar 1995. Bungee blunder *D.Telegraph* 12 Sept 1995. Cactus crush *Columbus Dispatch* 18 July 1986, *S.Express* 12 Nov 1995. Scout snuff *Rocky Mountains News* 7 June 1995. Dwarf death *Sun* 2 Oct 1995. Cricket croak *Sun* 3 Oct 1995. Hole-in-one horror *Lewiston, Maine Sun-Journal* 12 Nov 1994, *Toronto Sun* December 1995. Keep playing *D.Mirror* 30 Sept 1996. Getting a kick out of golf *Wolverhampton Express & Star* 23 Oct 1996. Posthumous supporter *Toronto Sun* 16 Nov 1995. Footie fracas *Aberdeen Press & Journal* 24 June 1994. Wrestlers in rubberwear *Guardian* 19 Dec 1997. Not a happy ending *People* 14 Nov 1993. Hooked *D.Mail* 17 Mar 1998. Southpaw survival *Guardian* 23 Dec 1994.

## CHAPTER 11: FIENDISH FUR AND FEATHERS

Well chicken *[AP]* 1 Aug 1995, *D.Telegraph* + *Hong Kong Express*, 13 April 1996. Rabbit zap *[AP]* 3 Mar 1995. Chicken feed *Times of Oman*, 19 Jan 1995. Flattened *[AP]* 23 Aug 1996, *Daily Telegraph*, *Express*, 1 Nov 1997. Man's best friend *Times*, *Daily Telegraph*, 30 Nov 1996, *Guardian*, 11 Dec 1996. Lion et *Guardian*, 11 Dec 1996, *D.Mirror* 11 Nov 1996. Lost language of dog *D.Telegraph* 16 Jan 1996. Don't shoot or the kitten gets it *[AP]* 22 Aug 1994. Cat massacre *[AP]* 12 May 1996. Mower massacre *[UPI]* 15 Oct 1997. Thanks a bunch *Victoria (BC) Times-Colonist*, 11 June 1997. Bird-lover *Sunday Express*, 1 Oct 1995, *[AP]* 29 Dec 1997. Killer peacock *[AP]* 4 April 1997. Python et *Express (Germany)* 3 April; *[AFP]* 7 April 1998, *Eastern Express*, 3 Feb; *Independent*, 4 Feb 1997. Back biting *[AFP]* 16 Oct 1996. Caterpillar death *[AFP]* 16 Oct 1996. Sheep strikes first *Sunday Telegraph*, 20 April 1997. Squirrel et *D.Mirror* 28 Jan 1993. Too much choke *E.Standard* 29 Aug 1979. Deer fall *Huddersfield Daily Examiner*, 10 Jan 1996. Iggy pop *Guardian* 14 Feb 1995.

Exterminator exterminated *Weekly News* 2 Mar 1996. Fright wig *S.Mail* (Scotland) 3 Mar 1996, *Eve. Herald* 27 Mar 1993, *People* 6 Feb 1994. Et dog *D.Record* 16 Apr 1996. Pig feed *D.Record* 19 Sept 1994. Bull stomp *Bangkok Post* 24 Jun 1994, *D.Mirror* 21 Mar 1994.

## CHAPTER 12: CRIME AND PUNISHMENT

Dog end *[AP]* 12 Oct 1994. Cash choke *Albuquerque Journal*, 29 April 1995; *Sydney Herald-Sun*, 2 Mar 1996. Flattened flashers *D.Record* 23 Oct 1995, *Sun* 1 Sept 1993. Todger trauma *D.Star* 16 Feb 1995. Own goal *People*, 27 Nov 1994. Glowing boss *The Sunday Mail (Brisbane)*, 28 Nov 1995. Convenient excuse *South China Morning Post*, 2 Feb 1996. Stiff door *D.Telegraph*, *D.Mail*, *Western Morning News*, 7 Nov 1995, *Edinburgh Eve. News*, 19 Mar 1996. Self-stewing *[AFP] Canberra Times*, 7 Jan 1996. Blind luck *Guardian*, 12 Oct 1996. DIY electric chair *[AP]*, *Philadelphia Daily News*, 3 Jan 1997; *[UPI]* 8 Mar 1988. Saved for slaughter *Independent* 16 Aug 1995. Spinach surprise *Guardian*, 22 May 1997. Cop shoots cop *The Times (of Malta)*, 11 Mar 1997, *USA Today* 26 Oct 1993. Asthma assassin *D.Mirror* 16 Sept 1994. Mutilators *Ziua* 25 Apr 1996. Corpse surprise *D.Record* 13 Aug 1994. Snow end *S.Mail* 17 Mar 1996, *D.Mirror* 25 Feb 1995. The Falls *Eve.Standard* 21 Aug 1996, *People* 24 Jul 1994. Double demise *D.Mail* 25 Oct 1995. Anger mismanagement *Victoria (BC) Times-Colonist* 14 Oct 1995.

## CHAPTER 13: DO IT YOURSELF

Have-a-go hero *D.Express*, 8 Oct 1993. Sawicide *Today*, 14 Dec 1992, *Sun* 10 Jun 1994. Gorge-ous *D.Record*, 31 Aug 1994, *San Diego Union-Tribune*, 3 Feb 1997. Serious drinking *D.Mirror*, 23 April 1997. Blaze of glory *South China Morning Post*, 29 Mar 1996, *[AP]* 4 June 1997. Blazing cock-ups *People*, 11 Dec 1994, *Sun*, 18 Mar 1992, *D.Telegraph*, 27 Nov 1993, *Observer*, 21 June 1992. Fiery fiasco *D.Star*, 20 May 1994; *People*, 29 May 1994. Cack-handed *D.Post* 20 Jan 1995. Animal exits *Aberdeen Press & Journal*, 1 Sept 1995, *New York Daily News*, 14 Mar 1994. Ghost wannabe *D.Telegraph*, 27 Dec 1997. Ear end *D.Telegraph*, 11 Sept 1997. Flying general *Akron Beacon Journal*, 13 May 1996. I'm bringing a friend *Toronto Sun*, 3 Feb 1998, *Halifax Evening Courier*, 1 Feb 1994. No, I'll do it *Sussex Eve. Argus* 6 Jan 1995. Stiff on a stick *Victoria (BC) Times-Colonist*, 17 Jan 1997. Give yourself a lift *Mirror*, 12 Mar 1998. For whom the bell doesn't toll *Eve.Standard*, 15 April 1998. Sick-le to death *Indian Express*, 20 Feb 1998. Scientific explanation *D.Record* 4 Oct 1996. Pipped to the post *D.Telegraph*, 14 Nov 1997, *D.Telegraph* 12 Feb 1981. Flying finish *D.Telegraph*, 24 Dec 1997. Two down ... *Aberdeen Evening Express*, 24 Mar 1997. ...Three to go *[R]* 27 Feb 1998. Toilet topper *Sussex Eve. Argus* 20 Aug 1996.

## CHAPTER 14: EAT, DRINK AND DIE MERRY

Bloater *Seattle Times*, 18 July; *Express*, 22 July *[AP]* 14 Aug 1997. Burst priest *Times* 29 Apr 1996, *Eve.News* 9 Jan 1974. Mochi massacre *New York Times International*, 4 Jan 1995; *Scotland on Sunday* 4 Jan 1998. Still dangerous *Nottingham Evening Post*, 8 Aug 1996, *D.Star* 15 Feb 1995. Table topped *Today*, 27 Dec 1993. Home-brew horror *Delict Magazin (Romania)*, April 1994. Just dropped in *Sun* 3 Dec 1994, *People* 14 Feb 1995, *The Monitor (Uganda)* 18 Jan 1995. Freezered *[R]* 29 May 1994, *D.Mirror* 14 Nov 1996, *D.Record* 16 Oct 1996. Killer cabbage *[AP]* 20 March 1996. Fake fart fatality *[AP]* 31 Aug 1995. Beet that *Independent* 22 Jun 1995. Poison pepper *ITV teletext*, 30 Nov 1996. And the toastmaster is toast! *Guardian*, 4 Mar 1997, *D.Mirror* 29 Mar 1995. Last suppers *Sun* 21 Feb 1992, *D.Star* 15 Oct 1994. Killer kegs *Guardian* 4 Jul 1995, *New York Post* 24 Nov 1993. Cryptozoological casualties *South China Morning Post*, 16 Jan 1994 *Today*, 27 Dec 1993, *D.Telegraph* 12 Jul 1995, *Independent* 31 May 1995. See-food Die-t *Omaha World Herald*, 4 Dec 1994. Fed-up *S.Express* 7 May 1995, *D.Record* 15 Jun 1995. Pickled *D.Mirror* 8 Sept 1995.

## CHAPTER 15: MOTORISED MAYHEM

Headless baby *[R]* 29 Nov 1996. In-car drowning *Meridien Record Journal*, 13 Aug 1994. Crusher *D.Mail*, 14 April 1997. Autostart atrocity *Globe and Mail (Toronto)*, 29 Oct 1997. Car attack *The Journal-Gazette (Fort Wayne, Indiana)*, 17 Nov 1994. Irritating noise *Kalamazoo Gazette*, 1 April 1995. Rabbit's revenge *Hong Kong Standard*, 8 Jan 1996. Musgrove's end *Los Angeles Times*, 17 Aug 1994. Lightning zap *[AP]* 26 July 1996. Topless taxidriver *Taxi Globe Trade*, Dec 1996. Tempting fate *London Eve. Standard*, 24 Mar 1997. Trapped *Philadelphia Daily News*, 22 July 1997, *S.Mail* 5 May 1996. Roo-kill *Evening Standard*, 22 Mar; *South China Morning Post*, 23 Mar 1996. Wheel freak *Nottingham Eve. Post* 17 Mar 1995. Chain-reaction *Independent on Sunday* 4 Sept 1994. Jacked off *San José Mercury* 7 Apr 1995. Arguing truckers *Sussex Eve. Argus* 20 Oct 1994. Tarmac'd *Manchester Eve. News* 27 Nov 1993. Dead man on the bus *People* 10 Sept 1995, *Guardian* 27 June 1995, *People* 16 Apr 1994. Negligent wardens *D.Telegraph* 23 Aug 1995, *Metropolitan Times* 26 Jan 1995.

## CHAPTER 16: LONG PORK

Ukrainian fry-up *[AP]* 5+9 June 1995. Really tasty *[R]* 2 Sept; *Sunday Times*, 10 Sept 1995. They ate their mate *[AP]* 8+25 July 1995; *[R]* 9 May 1996. Sebastapol slaughter *Rockland (NY) Journal News*, 27 Mar; *Times*, 28 Mar 1996. Canned husband *[AP]* 3 Oct 1995, *Coventry Eve. Telegraph*, 27 Nov 1995. Criminal ravioli *[AFP]* 8 Feb; *[R]* 9 Feb 1996. Son eater *Hong Kong Eastern Express*, 4 Mar 1996. Entrail grinder *Hong Kong Standard*, 12 July 1997, *Edinburgh Eve. News* 10 Nov 1994. Child eater *D.Record* 21 Oct 1994. Eat the rich *Western Daily Press* 24 Sept 1994. Lugora's lunch *D.Star* 12 Nov 1994.

## CHAPTER 17: NUMBER ONE IN A FIELD OF ONE

Treasure seeker *[R]* 6 July 1995. Deadly gamble *D.Telegraph*, 26 Feb 1996. Veteran cull *[R]* 11 Nov 1995. Death delay *S.Express*, 1 Oct 1995. Rabies returns *D.Mail*, 22 June 1996. Pheasant error *D.Telegraph*, 6 July 1996. Post death *[R]* 18 Sept 1997. Not a burglar *Halifax Evening Courier*, 10 Feb 1997. Blame the goat *South China Morning Post*, 7 Jan 1998. Both parents *Halifax Evening Courier*, 23 Oct 1996. Destiny ditch *NY Daily News* 16 Sept 1995. Hole horror *The Sunday Times (Brisbane)*, 10 Aug 1997. Eyeball park *S.Mail* 14 Aug 1994. More than he bargained for *News of the World* 22 Mar 1998. Cadaver cabby *New York Daily News* 6 Jan 1992. Motel corpses *[R]* 17 Aug 1994. Sprayed parts *D.Star* 22 Feb 1995. Nomadic Chinese dead *Guardian* 4 Nov 1995. Finnish finish *Guardian* 19 June 1996. Vain or what! *Western Mail*, 16 Feb 1995. Not Parvati *Ghatana Ra Bichar (Nepal)*, 13 Aug 1997. Fatal lipstick *Weekly News*, 23 Mar 1996, *D.Record*, 22 Aug 1997.

## CHAPTER 18: FINAL FIASCOS

Bog blast *[R]* 13 April 1998. Squat horror *L'Enquêteur (Ivory Coast)* 17 May 1993. Bog zap *Guardian*, *Western Mail*, 10 July; *Times* 12 July 1995. Electric shock *D.Telegraph*, 31 Mar 1997. Organ legs it *S.London Press* 1 Nov 1994. Tossed tot *Western Morning News*, 18 August 1993. Hydrant horror *D.Mirror* 21 June 1994. Final smoke *D.Express*, 15 May 1992. Sofa so dead *Augusta (Georgia) Chronicle*, 10 Jan 1994. Gum crash *Sun*, *D.Star*, 25 June 1994. Cliff collapse *D.Star*, 1 Sept; *Sun*, 8 Sept 1994. Karate klutz *D.Mail*, 17 Nov 1994. Oh Chute! *Augusta (GA) Chronicle*, 6 April 1994, *Atlanta Constitution*, 22 Sept 1992. Thai dies *Bangkok Post*, 6 Sept 1994, *[AP]* 18 Aug 1995, *Sun*, 20 May 1997. Porked *Sun*, 5 Dec 1996, *Mirror*, 8 Aug 1997. Well done *South China Morning Post*, 23 Sept 1996, *The Times (of Malta)*, 17 Oct 1997. No relief *The Citizen (South Africa)*, 1 Sept 1997. Final insult *Guardian* 14 May 1996. The lady vanishes *Sussex Eve. Argus* 10 Nov 1994, *Leics Mercury* 7 Apr 1995. Misdiagnosis *Guardian* 10 Nov 1995. Gross grave *Independent* 29 May 1996, *Coventry Eve.Telegraph* 19 Sept 1996.